6th edition

crossover

2

von
Peadar Curran

in Zusammenarbeit
mit der Verlagsredaktion

Ausgabe Baden-Württemberg
für berufliche Gymnasien

Workbook

KLASSE 12/13

Topic 1

Topic 2

Topic 3

Topic 4

Topic 5

Topic 6

Mock exam

Appendix

◁)) Dieses Symbol weist auf Hörtexte hin, die Sie in der PagePlayer-App finden. Laden Sie die kostenlose App herunter, wählen Sie **Crossover 6th edition Ausgabe Baden-Württemberg Band 2** aus und scannen Sie die jeweilige Seite bzw. rufen Sie den Hörtext im Medienmenü auf.

Dealing with visual material
p. 6 Do after Section D

Writing workshop 1
p. 8 Do after Section D

Getting to grips with grammar
p. 4 Do after Sections B & D

Writing workshop 2
p. 10 Do after Section A

Dealing with listening tasks
p. 12 Do after Section E

Words in context
p. 13

The chill out zone
p. 15

Getting to grips with grammar

Do after Section B

1   Participle constructions

G ▸ Participle constructions, SB, p. 296

Rewrite the sentences in your exercise book. Replace the <u>underlined</u> words with a present or a past participle. The first two have been done as examples.

1 Non-renewable energy sources are those <u>which are derived</u> from fossil fuels such as oil, coal and natural gas. *Non-renewable energy sources are those <u>derived</u> from fossil fuels …*

2 <u>As the sources take</u> millions of years to form, they are limited in quantity and at some point will run out. *<u>Taking</u> millions of years to form, they are limited …*

3 Mining these fuels causes terrible damage to the environment, <u>because it disturbs</u> ecosystems and <u>it harms</u> wildlife.

4 When <u>they are burned</u>, fossil fuels produce large amounts of pollution <u>which are known</u> as greenhouse gases, because they trap heat in the atmosphere.

5 <u>As they are alarmed</u> by climate change, environmentalists say the use of fossil fuels has to stop *now*.

6 <u>As it comes</u> from natural elements such as the sun, the wind or water, renewable energy will never run out and it is clean, <u>because it produces</u> no harmful emissions.

7 Nuclear energy does not create polluting gases, but the radioactive waste <u>which is left</u> behind will stay dangerous for thousands of years, <u>which means</u> future generations will have to deal with it.

4

Do after Section B

2 Gerund / Infinitive

G ▶ *Gerund/ Infinitive, SB, p. 292*

<u>Underline</u> the correct form, infinitive or gerund, of the verbs which follow the verbs in **bold**.

In London, the government **admitted** *to break / breaking* its promise not to grant more fracking licenses. The prime minister **denied** *to be / being* 'best friends' with the boss of one of the largest mining companies and he **avoided** *to answer / answering* a question about a possible link between fracking and a minor earthquake in the southwest of England last week. He did, however, **promise** *to look / looking* at the issue again. Meanwhile, environmental groups **hope** *to start / starting* a legal challenge against the new mining licenses in court tomorrow. The groups say that the UK cannot **afford** *to open / opening* one more new mine because the country already **risks** *to miss / missing* its climate change targets.

Do after Section D

3 The passive

G ▶ *The passive, SB, p. 290*

a   Rewrite these passive sentences as active sentences. Use a suitable subject from the box.

> bats • the Covid-19 pandemic • people in West Africa • Lassa fever
> • scientists and economists

1   Ebola was first passed on to humans in the 1970s.

2   Gorillas and chimpanzees were being slaughtered for food.

3   Trillions of dollars have been wiped from the global economy.

4   Between 300,000 and 500,000 people are infected in West Africa every year.

5   The cost of preventing future pandemics over the next ten years has been estimated to be 2% of the financial damage caused by Covid-19.

b   The passive is often used in formal writing to say what people believe or think. Rewrite the active sentences in the passive in the two ways shown below.

1   **People believe** that the Amazon rainforest produces 25% of the world's oxygen.

   i) **It + passive verb + that** → **It is believed that** *the Amazon rainforest produces 25% of ...*

   ii) **Subject + passive verb + to-infinitive** → *The Amazon rainforest* **is believed to produce** *25% of ...*

2   **They think** that the Amazon region is home to thirty million people.

3   **Experts estimate** that the Amazon rainforest loses tens of millions of hectares every year to farming, mining and oil extraction.

4   **Scientists have claimed** that a third of all emerging diseases are the result of changes in land use.

5   **People didn't expect** that the Covid-19 pandemic would last longer than a year.

6   **Medical experts have said** that Covid-19 and HIV share their origins in the close contact between people and wildlife.

Dealing with visual material

Do after Section D

1   Choose eight of the words / phrases below to label the images.

> draft • dull • expressive • juxtaposition • out of focus • outline • shaped like sth •
> silhouette • superimposed over • vague • vibrant

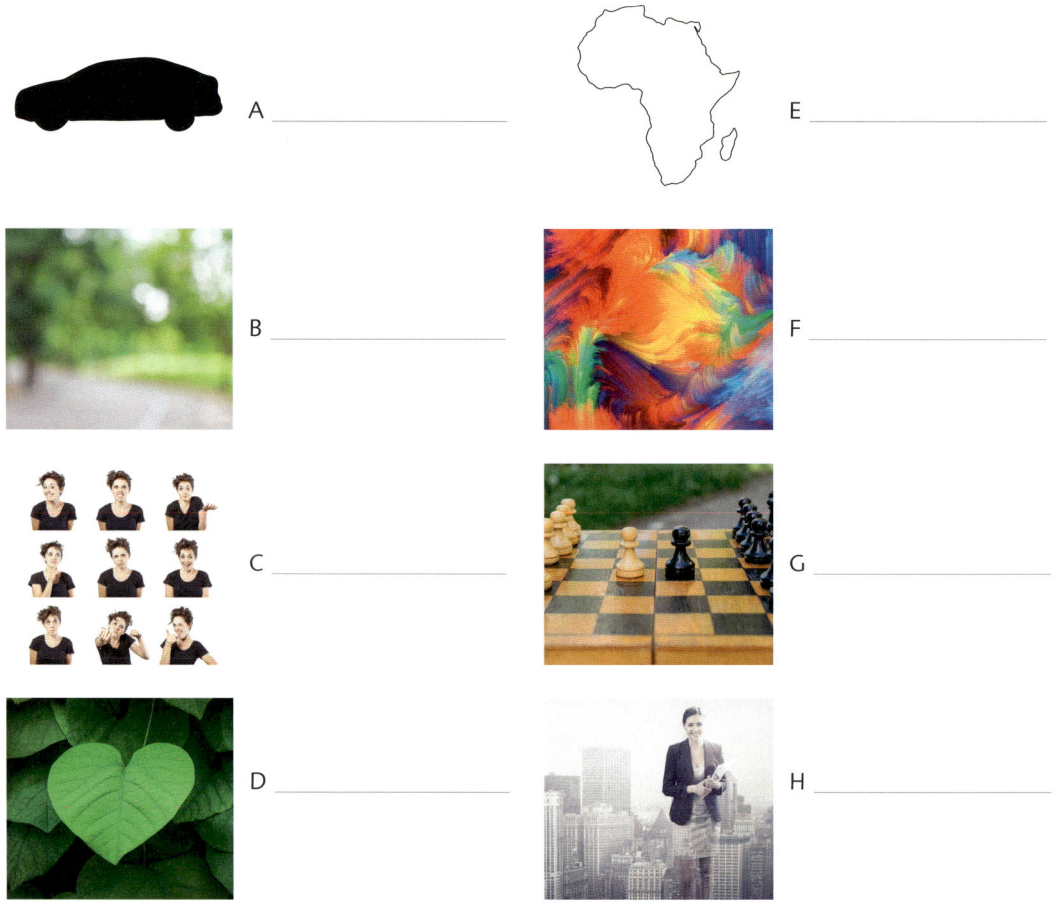

A _____   E _____

B _____   F _____

C _____   G _____

D _____   H _____

2   Examine this image for a minute. Note down what you see and what it makes you think of. Then do tasks a)–c).

"A nation that destroys its soils destroys itself. Forests are the lungs of our land, purifying the air and giving fresh strength to our people."
Franklin D. Roosevelt, US president 1933-45

a Describing an image

<u>Underline</u> the best alternative to complete the description of the image opposite.

TIP: In images containing *activity* – people or natural phenomenon such as animals, wind and rain, etc. – you should describe the activity with the present progressive. When there is no activity – as in this image – the simple present is appropriate.

At first sight, the image is a/an *cartoon / infographic / photo* of a large area of countryside with a *speech / quotation / citation* superimposed over it. On closer inspection, however, it is clear the forested areas in the *centre / background / foreground* of the image are *figures / forms / shaped* like a pair of human lungs. There are paths leading to and also going into the 'lungs' which *resemble / reflect / remind* parts of our breathing system. The top part of the 'lung' *on / in / at* the right is brown where it *is appearing / appears / has appeared* the trees have been cut down. The area of land *wrapping / circling / surrounding* the upper part of both 'lungs' is barren, pale brown and *looking / is looking / looks* like a desert.

At / In / On the bottom of the photo, there is a white box superimposed over the image which *stands / says / read* "A nation that destroys its soils destroys itself. Forests are the lungs of our land, purifying the air and giving fresh strength to our people." Former US president Franklin D. Roosevelt is the source of the *speech / quotation / citation*.

b Interpreting an image

Complete the analysis of the image with the correct forms of the verbs below. Use every verb.

> alter • cause • convey • evoke • help • reinforce

Obviously, the image has been 1.＿＿＿＿＿＿＿＿＿＿ by computer to achieve its suggestion of human lungs. The desert area around the 'lungs' could have been 2. ＿＿＿＿＿＿＿＿＿＿ by logging, for instance. The left 'lung' 3. ＿＿＿＿＿＿＿＿＿＿ the impression of disease – lung cancer, perhaps. One can't 4. ＿＿＿＿＿＿＿＿＿＿ linking human activity to the diseased lung – it is people who have caused this disease. Roosevelt's statement 5. ＿＿＿＿＿＿＿＿＿＿ this message: the soil in the image has been destroyed and, as a consequence, humanity's 'lungs' are also being affected negatively. The images of nature and Roosevelt's statement 6. ＿＿＿＿＿＿＿＿＿＿ the clear connection between our own physical health and the health of the environment, especially forests.

c Evaluating an image

Your own opinion is important in evaluating an image. You must state why you think an image is effective / ineffective in conveying its message.

Write an evaluation in your exercise book. You can base your evaluation on a) and b) above.

Support your view by saying which elements of the image are responsible for it being successful or unsuccessful.

How to say it or write it

In my opinion, the image is effective / ineffective in conveying its message because (of) …

The combination of … and … is (not very) powerful / thought-provoking / makes you stop and think.

The written message echoes / does not echo the message conveyed by the image.

The contrast / juxtaposition of vibrant colours / healthy trees and the barren / desolate land is particularly effective / does not quite work.

Writing workshop 1

Do after Section D

Knowing about rhetorical and structural devices, imagery and sound devices can help you analyse texts in your exam, and also improve your creative writing. In these pages, we will examine these devices and why they are used.

1 Read this sample answer to the speech writing exercise 8 on page 25 of your student's book.

Good afternoon, ladies and gentlemen,

It may be the case that some of **A** <u>you</u> are here today because of BetterBuy's beef sale. **B** <u>BetterBuy says</u> that you want quality food at low prices, but what **B** <u>they don't say</u> is that this food comes at the highest price there is!

We are protesting here today because **A** <u>you</u> need to know that **C** <u>BetterBuy is selling</u> food grown   5
on land that used to be part of the Amazon rainforest. **C** <u>They are selling</u> beef from cows that eat grass where there was once lush forest and wildlife. **C** <u>They are selling</u> it because we are *buying* it. **A** <u>They</u> say it is quality food, but we must also take into account *quality of life*.

Let me tell you what I mean. The Amazon rainforest is the **D** <u>lungs</u> of the Earth, and a home to people and indigenous tribes. Those **D** <u>living walls of wood and its roof of green leaves</u> shelter 30%   10
of the world's animal and plant species. Despite this, millions of hectares of rainforest are being bulldozed every year **E** <u>to grow grass</u> for cattle to graze, **E** <u>to cultivate crops</u> and **E** <u>to mine for minerals</u>. Nearly one-fifth of these life-giving lungs has already been destroyed. In the face of climate change, we *need* these forests to survive. And it really is a question of survival: scientists say there is evidence that deforestation, destruction of wild habitats and the change in land use   15
increase the chances of more pandemics. Save a few pennies today, but **F** <u>the price</u> which we have to pay could be a pandemic tomorrow. We need to ask ourselves – **G** <u>can we afford it</u>?

H <u>I only came here to do my shopping – I hear you say; what can one person do? – I hear you wonder;</u> I can't change the world – that's where you're wrong. You – and the money in your pocket – are more powerful than you presume, and you are *not* alone. Our organization is here to   20
help. We can inform you about the products which come from the Amazon and show you alternatives that are not expensive and do not have the same harmful environmental effects. All we ask is that you give us a few minutes of your time.

Together, **A** <u>we</u> can stop supermarkets like BetterBuy selling beef from the Amazon. If **A** <u>we</u> don't buy it, **A** <u>they</u> won't sell it. Remember! **I** <u>If we all make small changes to what we buy and how we</u>   25
<u>live</u>, they will all add up to a better tomorrow for everyone and our planet.

Thank you.   (438 words)

Look at your student's book pages 211–212 and the PagePlayer App for more help.

2 The speaker uses a number of techniques in the speech. Match the letters A-I of the <u>underlined</u> parts of the speech with the device or technique in the table below.

Rhetorical devices: _A_ use of pronouns, _____ contrast/antithesis, _____ rhetorical questions

Structural devices: _____ parallelism, _____ concluding call to action / appeal, _____ repetition/anaphora

Imagery: _____ metaphors, _____ symbolism

Sound devices: _____ alliteration

3   The following analysis of the speech is longer than usual because it examines all nine of the devices used in the speech.
Complete it with the name of the device or technique from exercise 2.

This speech was given at a protest outside a supermarket. As the function of the speech was to convince the audience that buying food from the Amazon was dangerous for the environment, the tone was serious.

The _use of pronouns_, especially addressing the audience directly with 'you', is an effective way of showing them that they should be on the speaker's side. The pronoun 'we' is then used to convey   5 how the speaker and the audience can act together. Furthermore, using 'they' to refer to the supermarket gets the message across to the audience that the supermarket is on the opposite side of the argument.

The speech contains many devices that help to make the speaker's message memorable. For example, the use of 1. _____ in "BetterBuy says ..., but what they don't say ..."   10 (ll. 2–4) contrasts the two sides of the argument, making the audience think the supermarket is not telling the whole truth while the speaker is honest. The use of 2. _____ in the repetition of "BetterBuy is selling ... They are selling ... They are selling" (ll. 5–7) gives the speech a rhythm and allows the speaker to emphasize the message.

As a speech is a spoken text, sound is an important part of an effective speech. This can be seen   15 in the many examples of alliteration in the speech: the repetition of the 'gr' sound in "grow", "grass" and "graze" (l. 12) or the 'c' in "cultivate" and "crops" (l. 12) to give two examples. To add to the rhythm and sound, the speaker also employs imagery. The 3. _____ used, e.g. "lungs", "living walls" help the audience to picture the speaker's words in their minds. This combined with the 4. _____ of the possible "price" they could have to pay, helps   20 to make a strong impression on the listeners.

By the middle of the speech, the audience understands the impact that the destruction of the Amazon rainforest has on the environment. After giving so much information, there is a risk of losing the audience's attention, so the speaker employs a 5. _____ to keep them interested. This device encourages the audience to reflect on the answer but assumes they will   25 agree with the speaker anyway, thus making the argument more convincing. The speaker uses 6. _____ by repeating "I hear you" in "I hear you say" and "I hear you won-der" and then challenges the listeners by telling them they are wrong if they think they cannot change anything.

The speaker explains that his/her organization is there to help the audience and lists solutions to   30 the problem raised at the beginning. The speech finishes with a call to action in the form of an imperative to "Remember!" and reaches a positive 7. _____ with an optimistic promise of a "better tomorrow".

4   Look back over the speech you wrote for exercise 8 on page 25 of your student's book.
Improve it by using some of the devices from these pages.

9

Writing workshop 2

Do after Section A

Look at your student's book pages 167–172 and the PagePlayer App for more help.

The human impact on the environment

In these pages you will work on writing an argumentative text (written discussion).

1 A reader of the Young Globe has written a letter to the magazine's editor in response to the Conversation Corner article (student's book, pages 11–12). Read the letter and sum up the writer's opinion in 2–3 sentences in your exercise book.

Madam,

I read with interest this month's 'Conversation Corner' and I am writing to you today to express my disagreement with the whole premise of the article.

Firstly, I do not think that it is helpful to spend time explaining to people what a geological epoch is, even less how the dinosaurs became extinct. Will that knowledge encourage people to recycle more or drive their cars less? No, it will not.

Secondly, changing the name of our current epoch from Holocene to Anthropocene is, in my opinion, not going to act as a 'wake-up call'. Governments and people do not pay attention to these labels, and people who do not believe in man-made climate change do not listen to scientific experts in any case. Changing one word will make no difference at all to people's behaviour and that is what must change.

Finally, your interviewer and interviewee talked about humanity's impact on the environment: plastic waste, wildlife extinction and deforestation, but the only statement the interviewer could make at the end was to express the *hope* that the 'Anthropocene' can be a new age for humanity and the environment. There was no mention of any practical steps that people can take to achieve this 'positive new age'.

In conclusion, I would ask your magazine to spend less time discussing irrelevant labels that no one pays attention to and less time talking about the damage that has already been done to our planet. Instead, please spend more time focusing on concrete action that people can take to turn your interviewer's 'hope' into reality.

Shane Keogh, Cork

2 In a written discussion, it is helpful to know phrases and words that a) combine supporting arguments or b) contrast opposing arguments.
Complete the table with the English translations from the box.

despite the fact that • ~~furthermore~~ • in addition (to) • moreover • nevertheless • not only … but also • on the contrary • on the one hand … on the other hand • similarly • whereas

a. Combining supporting arguments		b. Contrasting opposing arguments	
darüber hinaus	*furthermore*	im Gegensatz dazu	
nicht nur …, sondern auch		nichtsdestotrotz	
ähnlich		während/wogegen/indessen	
überdies/ferner		trotz der Tatsache, dass	
zusätzlich (zu)		einerseits … anderseits	

3 Look at the following task:

"By naming the current epoch the Anthropocene, we can acknowledge the impact human beings have had on the planet and emphasize our great responsibility to take care of our one, and only, home."
Discuss the pros and cons of taking the action described in the quotation.

a Now look at the points below. Decide if they are 'pro' or 'con'.

people who are sceptical of man-made climate change won't care about changing one scientific name   _____

the Anthropocene is based on hard facts and we should use every piece of evidence to convince people to care about our planet   _____

If you changed the name of cocaine or heroin to 'poison', would it stop people taking drugs? No.   _____

some newspapers use the words 'heating' and 'crisis' instead of 'warming' and 'change' – words have power   _____

nobody cares about these strange names; they worry about today's and tomorrow's problems   _____

we need to educate people about how we are affecting the planet and declaring a new epoch could be part of that education   _____

b Use five of the points from a) to complete this comment on the task. Then write your own opinion in the conclusion.

It has been suggested that we should name our current geological epoch the Anthropocene in order to emphasize the enormous impact humanity has had on our environment and our responsibility as guardians of our fragile planet. In this comment, I will examine some potential benefits of and some reasons against taking this action.

On the one hand, supporters say the Anthropocene name _____

_____. On the other hand, _____

_____.

Supporters say on the contrary, _____

_____ and this power can influence not only people's

opinions but also government policies. Nevertheless, it could be argued that _____

_____ instead.

Despite the fact that Anthropocene is just a word, renaming our epoch can be part of a learning

process; _____

_____.

In conclusion, having looked at both sides of the argument, my own view is _____

_____

_____

_____

_____

11

Dealing with listening tasks

Do after Section E

Sustainable fashion

Look at your student's book pages 123–125 and the PagePlayer App for more help.

Task type: Matching

In this type of task, you have to match some short headings to the correct speaker, but you must be careful because there will be some extra headings that you do not need.

1   Read the listening task at the bottom of the page carefully. Take 1–2 minutes to look up any words you do not understand. Then, before you listen, do exercises 2 and 3 below.

2   Tick the descriptions which you think are relevant to this type of task.

In this task, I need to …

a   listen for exact details such as numbers and statistics. ☐

b   understand every word in the headings which are given. ☐

c   understand every word the speakers say. ☐

d   understand the speakers' general opinions and listen to their tone. ☐

e   think about what I know about the topic. ☐

f   complete the task after listening to the audio once. ☐

3   Fast fashion is the topic of the listening task. Circle the vocabulary in the box that is relevant to the topic. Thinking about the topic will help 'activate' your background knowledge.

> etiquette • child labour • renewables • sustainable • throw-away culture • organic food • the third world • suppliers • fossil fuels • sweatshops • lend/borrow clothes • charity shops

4   Now it is time to do the listening task.

You will hear five speakers give their views on so-called fast fashion. While listening, match the headings A to G with the speakers 1 to 5. There are two more headings than you need.
You now have time to read the assignment.

	Heading			
A	Overcome with apathy	**E**	Fast fashion is just media hype
B	A convert to the sharing economy	**F**	Looks are everything
C	Sustainable fashion is a fraud	**G**	Fashion designers are to blame
D	Consumerism is the real problem		

Speaker	1	2	3	4	5
Heading					

Now listen to the recording again.

Words in context

1 Read this article about the younger and older generations' attitudes to the environment.

Generation Greenwash:
are the young really as 'eco' as they think they are?

Saving the planet. Eco-activism. Passionate public protest. It's an age and stage thing; the preserve of the young and idealistic. Or so it used to be. But something has shifted. Here in 21st century Britain, the typical eco-warrior has a different face – very often attached to a middle-aged man and glued to the M25.

5 While the nation's teenagers are dumping their tents at music festivals, stockpiling plastic food delivery containers and swelling the coffers of online fast fashion retailers, it is their parents – and grandparents – who are stepping up to the crease, clamouring for change and, crucially, taking personal responsibility.

[...] A Government report [...] acknowledged that young people were more likely to go vegan, or
10 vegetarian, but pulled no punches in other respects. "Gen Z are more likely to say they care about the environment compared to other generations, though there is a relatively small difference between their views and those of millennials," it said. But while Gen Z have strongly stated beliefs, it continued, "these do not necessarily translate into action – for example, they do not necessarily recycle, despite expressing their environmental concerns."

15 [...] That doesn't mean there is no place for speaking out. Pre-pandemic, Extinction Rebellion's school strikes saw thousands of pupils stage walkouts in order to convey their distress and dismay at climate change. But that moment has passed and instead the oldies at Insulate Britain are continuing their immensely irritating – ergo, highly effective – campaign of traffic disruption in order to raise awareness of the [...] loss of heat from poorly insulated UK homes. [...] Meanwhile,
20 their kids and grandkids are holed up in their bedrooms, living their best lives online. Climate change appears to be of vanishingly little interest compared with cinnamon toast hacks and editing selfies so you look like you're on the cover of Vogue magazine.

[Our children] might piously badger us to buy an electric car but they have no ethical qualms about cadging lifts in the family gas-guzzler. And for every 30-something millennial worrying
25 about the food miles racked up by her avocado (but still buying it), there's a Gen Zer blaming Big Government for everything. "My 16-year-old son is vegan, and literally believes it gives him a free pass to do anything he pleases," admits my friend Kathryn, an administrator from the Midlands. [...] "When I pointed out that the mass production of his latest new trainers is so environmentally damaging that it comes third behind aviation and shipping, he was furious," she says.

30 Kathryn is right. Trainers cause 1.4 per cent of global greenhouse gas emissions. To put that into context, aviation causes 2.5 per cent. It's baffling until you drill down into the deeply disturbing detail. "There are 25 billion pairs of running shoes made every year – enough to go round the earth 300 times – and most made from plastic," says Angela Terry, an environmental scientist and founder of consumer advice company One House.

35 [...] But when it comes to adjusting the mindset of young people, Terry believes transparency and information rather than shame or guilt are the keys to conversion. "In the words of the UN, we need rapid, far-reaching, unprecedented change across the whole of society," she says. "In order to do that, the generations must pull together, not engage in the blame game. There's far too much at stake to leave anyone behind."
40 Let us hope that Generation Greenwash agrees.

(568 words)   Source: *The Telegraph*, 2 November 2021

eco- *(ecological)* Öko-

M25 *eine Autobahn, die um London herumführt*

to **dump sth** *etw abladen*

to **stockpile** *aufstapeln*

to **swell the coffers** *die Kassen auffüllen*

to **step up to the crease** *etw in die Hand nehmen*

to **clamour for sth** *nach etw schreien*

crucially *entscheidend*

to **acknowledge** *bestätigen*

to **pull no punches** *sich nicht zurückhalten*

respect *(hier) Beziehung*

not **necessarily** *nicht unbedingt*

to **stage sth** *(hier) etw veranstalten*

distress *Kummer*

dismay *Entsetzen*

irritating *ärgerlich*

ergo *demzufolge*

disruption *Belästigung*

to **hole up** *sich eingraben*

vanishingly *verschwindend*

piously *fromm*

to **badger sb** *jdn plagen*

qualms *Bedenken*

to **cadge sth from sb** *jdn anpumpen für etw*

gas-guzzler *Benzinfresser*

to **rack up sth** *etw erzielen, einbringen*

aviation *Luftfahrt*

baffling *rätselhaft*

to **drill down (into sth)** *nachforschen*

to **pull together** *am gleichen Strang ziehen*

blame game *gegenseitige Schuldzuweisungen*

to **be at stake** *auf dem Spiel stehen*

2   You can find the highlighted words from the text on page 13 in the table below.
    Fill in the empty boxes in the following wordlist.

Word/Phrase	Memory support	German
_____	**COLLOCATIONS** to lay the ~ (for sth) on sb/sth to place the ~ (for sth) on sb/sth to play the ~ game to be to ~ for sth to bear the ~	Schuld
belief	**WORD FAMILY** to (dis-)_____ (vb) (dis-)belief (n) _____ (n) (dis-) _____ (adj) (un-)_____ (adj) (un-)believably (adv)	Glaube, Meinung
environment	**WORD FAMILY** environment (n) _____ (adj) _____ (adv)	Umwelt
_____	**COLLOCATIONS** ~ activism, activist, efficient, (un)friendly, minded, movement sensitive, warrior	Öko-
emission	**WORD FAMILY** to _____ (vb) emission (n)	Ausstoß
_____	**SENTENCE:** Carbon dioxide is called a _____ because it traps the heat of the sun in our atmosphere and contributes to global warming.	Treibhausgas

3   Match the idioms from the text with the correct definition.

Idiom

1 to step up to the crease (or plate)

2 to not pull any / your punches

3 to hole up / be holed up

4 to badger somebody (into doing something)

5 to leave somebody behind

Definition

a to speak in a direct and honest way even if it sounds unkind or harsh

b to make much better progress than somebody

c to keep annoying somebody until they do want you want

d to do what is needed in the case of an opportunity or a crisis

e to stay, shelter or hide in a place

The chill out zone

1 **Who said that?**
Match these real quotations about climate change and the environment with the correct speaker.

1 At the COP26 climate conference in 2021:

"You can shove your climate crisis up your arse!"

A Greta Thunberg

2 About wind energy in 2022:

"The windmills, they don't work, they're too expensive, they kill all the birds, ruin the landscapes."

B Elon Musk

3 About renewable energy, 2022:

"Obviously the sun only shines during the day, and sometimes it is very cloudy. So you need solar batteries. That will be the main long-term way that civilization is powered."

C Donald Trump

4 About dealing with waste, June 2019:

"I'm thinking about organizing a little beach cleanup for all the hotties. Y'all gotta come in y'all bikinis and clean up some shit!"

D Angela Merkel

5 About climate change, July 2021:

"We have to hurry, we have to get faster in the fight against climate change."

E Megan Thee Stallion

2 **Prefixes and suffixes**
Add a prefix and a suffix to a word core to complete eight words from Topic 1.
Use each part once. One has been done for you.

Prefix	Word core	Suffix		Word
de	consump	able	1	*deforestation*
dis	cycl	able	2	
over	ethic	able	3	
pre-	**forest**	al	4	
re	lov	**ation**	5	
re	new	ed	6	
un	pos	ed	7	
un	treat	tion	8	

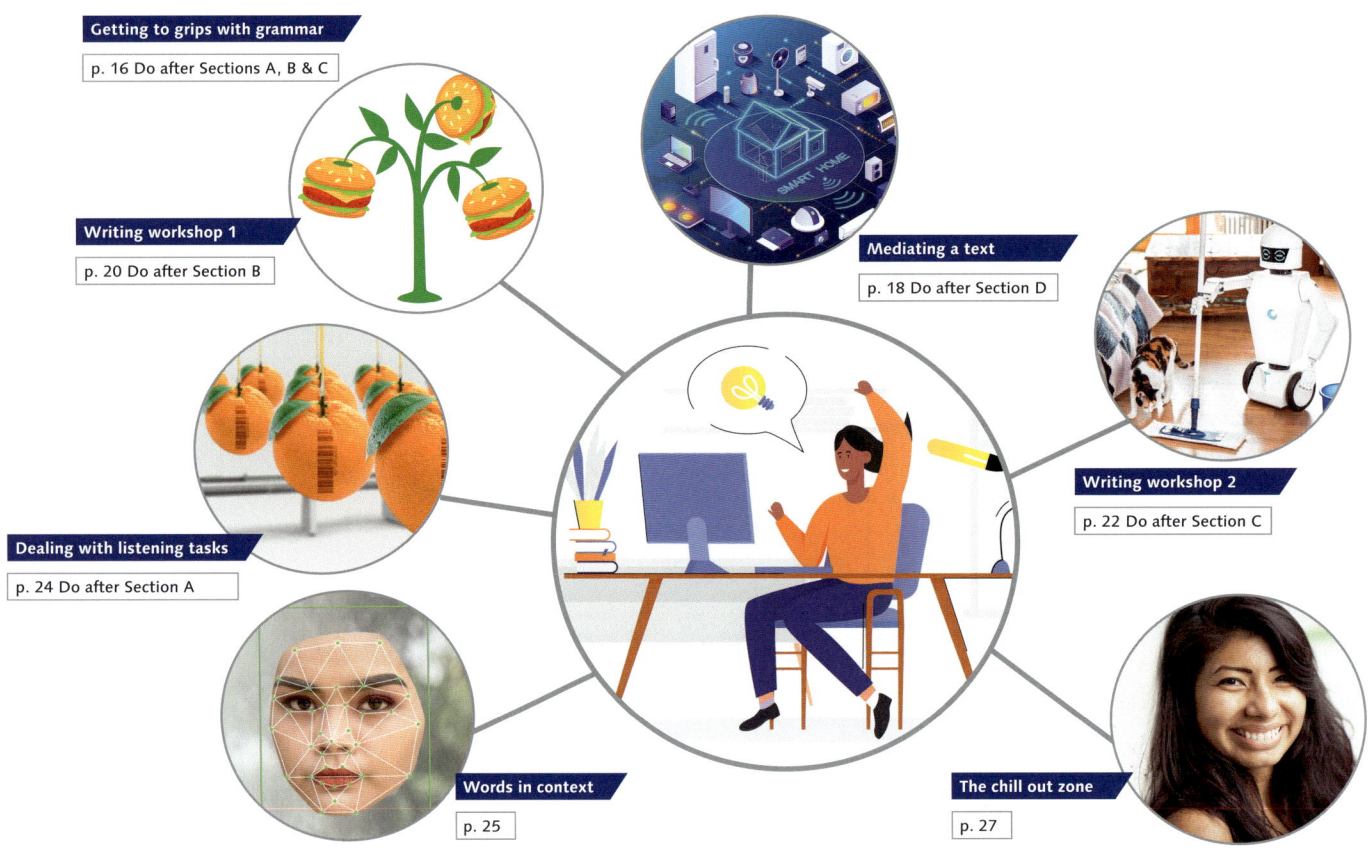

Getting to grips with grammar
p. 16 Do after Sections A, B & C

Writing workshop 1
p. 20 Do after Section B

Mediating a text
p. 18 Do after Section D

Writing workshop 2
p. 22 Do after Section C

Dealing with listening tasks
p. 24 Do after Section A

Words in context
p. 25

The chill out zone
p. 27

Getting to grips with grammar

Do after Section A

G ▶ Participle constructions, SB, p. 296

1 Participle constructions

Rewrite the sentences in your exercise book. Replace the underlined clause with a perfect participle clause so that the new sentence begins with 'Having …', as in the example.

1 Scientists created the first GMO, a modified bacteria, in 1973 <u>after they had identified the structure of DNA twenty years before</u>.

Having identified the structure of DNA twenty years before, scientists created the first GMO …

2 The first consumer GMO, a genetically engineered human insulin to treat diabetes, went on sale in 1982 <u>after it had received approval from the US FDA</u>.

3 The sale of GMO foods became more widespread in the US in the 1990s <u>after it had begun with GM tomatoes in 1994</u>.

4 Genetic engineering was first approved in an animal, salmon, for human consumption in 2015 <u>after it had been used in a variety of crops</u>.

5 The FDA began considering the next step in GMO science – editing the genes of organisms themselves – in 2019 <u>after it had accumulated over 25 years of experience in GMO foods</u>.

6 The EU has gradually expanded the range of GMOs cultivated and sold in its member states – <u>it had only allowed one GM corn crop for many years</u>, but it is still far behind the US.

Do after Section B

2 Reported speech

G ▶ Reported speech, SB, p. 288

Below, you will find some quotations from a podcast which was broadcast some months ago. In your exercise book, report what the interviewer and the guest said.

1 Lori: This edition of our podcast is interesting to me as a steak-lover as it will focus on plant-based meat.

Lori said that that edition of their podcast was interesting to her as a steak-lover as it would focus on …

2 Lori: Here to talk with me today is the Head of PR of Vegan World.

3 Lori: What steps are you taking to make eating vegetarian more appealing?

4 Simon: We've found that a big part of the problem now is how plant-based meat is marketed.

5 Lori: What do you mean?

6 Simon: Up until now, most marketing has presented the product as "meat-free", but we've found this to be very ineffective.

7 Simon: It makes people focus on what they're not getting. It's important that the consumers can focus on what they are getting.

8 Lori: Can you give me an example of this?

9 Simon: We decided to try out a few different names and it made a huge difference.

Do after Section C

3 Relative clauses

G ▶ Relative clauses, SB, p. 295

Decide if the sentences below contain a defining or non-defining clause. Add commas to the sentences with non-defining clauses. One has been done for you.

1 The abbreviation AI _,_ which was first coined in 1955 _,_ stands for artificial intelligence.

2 Dogs _____ which were first domesticated between twenty and forty thousand years ago _____ will never be replaced by robots in their roles as assistants to blind people or therapy animals.

3 During the Covid-19 pandemic in Singapore, robot dogs _____ that were programmed to make sure people socially distance _____ frightened children and older people.

4 The world's first AI-powered robot artist Ai-Da _____ which was named after the mathematician Ada Lovelace _____ hosted its own art exhibition at Oxford University in 2019.

5 Last year, however, Ai-Da _____ which uses cameras for eyes _____ was stopped and held for ten days at an Egyptian airport because police feared it was a spying device.

6 A Wittenberg church introduced a robot _____ that beamed lights from its hand to give blessings to people _____ to mark the 500th anniversary of the publication of Martin Luther's Theses.

7 Microsoft had to shut down an artificially intelligent chatbot called Tay because it made racist and sexist comments _____ that it had learned from humans.

8 Microsoft's CEO said the incident _____ which happened in 2016 _____ was a valuable learning experience as today's AI chatbots are a normal part of online customer service systems.

Mediating a text: From German to English

Look at your
student's
book pages
257–259
and the
PagePlayer
App for
more help.

Do after Section D

When mediating a text from one language to another, it is very important to avoid translating word-for-word. Let's look at two reasons why.

1 True friends and false friends. Some German and English words are cognates – they look similar and have similar meanings, but others are false friends – they look similar but have different meanings.
In the table below, write in the English word that has the same meaning as the German word. German words in green have English cognates, while the red words have false friends in English – be careful with those.

jdn/etw kontrollieren	*to check sb/sth*	von jdm/etw profitieren	*to profit from sb/sth*
etw studieren	*to study sth*	eventuell	
etw recherchieren		etw organisieren	
aktuell		sensibel	
etw bekommen		also	

2 Figurative language. Idioms, metaphors and similes often don't make sense when translated literally, so it is good to practise paraphrasing the core meaning of such phrases and expressions. Do this with the two English and two German expressions below. For the English expressions, write the meaning in German and for the German, write in English. One has been done for you.

a to put the cart before the horse:

  Dinge in der falschen Reihenfolge tun

b to pour cold water on sth:

c den Kopf in den Sand stecken:

d seinen Senf dazugeben:

3 It is always important to analyse the mediation task carefully. Analyse the task in exercise 4 by filling in the table below. This will help you to decide the form and content for the next step.

Audience	Text type	Aim	Register	Content

4   Now, do the mediation task in your exercise book.

Your class is doing a joint project with a school in Ireland on the Internet of Things. There is a website with two sections: Opportunities and Risks. For the 'Risks' section of the website, summarize in English the author's perspective on smart homes and data privacy and protection.

Ein sicheres Smart Home ist nur so sicher wie sein schwächstes Glied: du selbst

Wer zu dem Drittel der deutschen Haushalte gehört, die von einem intelligenten Zuhause träumen, oder zu den vierzig Prozent, die darüber nachdenken, ihr Haus zu vernetzen, muss nicht unbedingt Schlimmes befürchten, sollte sich aber bewusst sein, welche möglichen Schäden dem Nutzen gegenüber stehen.

5   Intelligente Beleuchtungssysteme können den Anschein erzeugen, als sei jemand zu Hause, auch wenn das Haus leer ist. Wer gerade unterwegs ist, kann mittels Video-Türklingeln problemlos sehen, wer an der Tür steht. Aber nicht alle Einbrecher sind ahnungslos. Man muss kein Genie sein, um die automatischen Muster intelligenter Beleuchtungssysteme zu durchschauen, und mit ein bisschen Geduld und Aufmerksamkeit können diese intelligenten Lichter eine Ein-
10   ladung sein: „Hey! Das Licht ist an, aber niemand ist zu Hause!" Und was die Video-Türklingeln angeht: Wenn Europa dem amerikanischen Vorbild folgt, was durchaus vorstellbar ist, können die Bilder der Kamera schon bald an die örtliche Polizeistation gesendet werden.

Ebenso attraktiv wie die Möglichkeiten, die eigene Wohnung sicherer zu machen, ist ein anderer Vorzug des Smart Home: der Komfort. Geht die Milch zur Neige, bestellt der Kühlschrank ein-
15   fach neue. Wird das Waschmittel knapp, sorgt die Waschmaschine dafür, dass am nächsten Tag neues geliefert wird. Klingt perfekt – wer muss sich bei einer solchen Ausstattung noch auf den Weg zum Supermarkt machen. Ähnlich wie bei „wearables", also tragbaren Computersystemen wie Gesundheitscheckern, liegen die Vorteile auf der Hand. Wer allerdings glaubt, dass Technologieunternehmen diese intelligenten Geräte nur entwickeln, um unser Leben besser zu machen,
20   läuft Gefahr, sich leichtsinnig gigantischen Datenbanken auszuliefern. Big Tech sammelt riesige Mengen an Daten über uns, die, selbst wenn sie anonymisiert werden, ein Netz strukturierter Informationen über menschliche Gewohnheiten und Verhaltensweisen aufbauen. Wir gewähren ihnen Einblicke in unser Privatleben, so dass sie genau wissen, wie sie uns ansprechen können – und zwar genau dann, wenn wir am empfänglichsten für verlockende Impulskäufe sind.

25   Die Smart-Home-Revolution führt langsam aber sicher dazu, dass wir mehr und mehr unserer intimsten Daten in die Hände anderer geben. Und sie geben sie weiter, denn – so will man uns glauben machen – wenn Smart Homes funktionieren sollen, müssen die Geräte verschiedener Hersteller miteinander kommunizieren können. Das erklärt aber nicht, warum ein Hersteller intelligenter Staubsauger die Daten über den Grundriss der Wohnungen seiner Kunden zu Mar-
30   ketingzwecken an Drittunternehmen weitergibt, wie die deutschen Datenschutzbehörden vor ein paar Jahren feststellten. Sobald wir unsere Daten weitergeben, geben wir auch die Verantwortung für ihren Schutz ab. Sie fließen durch die Netzwerke der Unternehmen und werden in ihren Clouds gespeichert. Wenn ihre Sicherheit von Hackern angegriffen wird, ist auch unsere persönliche Sicherheit gefährdet.

35   Dies ist von allen Risiken das größte: die Gefährdung unserer persönlichen Sicherheit. Eine Studie hat ergeben, dass nur 34 % der deutschen Smart-Home-Besitzer befürchten, ihr Haus könnte gehackt werden. Das bedeutet, dass fast zwei Drittel von ihnen die Augen vor diesem Risiko verschließen. Die wenigsten von ihnen wissen, wie sie ihr Heim-WLAN sicher verschlüsseln und schützen können. Nur jeder Zweite macht sich Sorgen um den Datenschutz – und das in einer
40   Gesellschaft, in der die Privatsphäre ein hohes Gut darstellt. Zur Wahrheit gehört nämlich auch, dass viele vor lauter Begeisterung für Technologie und Bequemlichkeit die mühsamen Prozeduren für Sicherheit und Datenschutz überspringen, etwa die Zwei-Faktor-Authentifizierung oder das Lesen von Nutzungsvereinbarungen vor dem Anklicken des „Einverstanden"-Kästchens. Intelligente Systeme sind nur so sicher wie ihr schwächstes Glied, und das sind in den meisten
45   Fällen wir.   (558 Wörter)

Writing workshop 1

Look at your
student's
book pages
213–218
and the
PagePlayer
App for
more help.

Do after Section B

First, read the text opposite, then do exercises 1–6.

1 Text function: What is the author's aim? To inform, to argue the pros and cons of the topic or to persuade the reader of her point of view? Give examples from the text to support your answer. TIP: A text can have more than one aim.

2 Register: State the register (formal, informal, neutral) used in the text, give evidence to support your answer and say why you think the author chose it.

3 Types of argument: Link the five types of argument with the correct description and then with an example of the argument from the text. One has been done for you.

Type of argument	Description	Examples from the text
a practical argument	**1** rebuttal of a counter-argument	*i.* Who can argue with a win-win proposition like that?
b argument by authority	**2** link to shared values	*ii.* By farming animals for meat, we are like the asteroid that wiped out the dinosaurs …
c normative argument	**3** comparison of dissimilar things	*iii.* Our products are too expensive [...] because we're small right now [...] we need your support to grow …
d argument by analogy	**4** verifiable statements of fact	*iv.* Top experts estimate regrowth of biomass would suck 800 thousand billion tons of CO_2 from the air …
e indirect argument	**5** evidence from research or reputable third-parties	*v.* … our products have the appearance, taste and texture of the foods [meat-lovers] adore – we know that because they've told us!

4 Text structure: Choose the right words from the box to describe how the text is structured.

> appeals • cause and effect • conclusion • descriptive • engages •
> explains • orders • poses • present • problem • solutions

The text structure 1. _____ the reader in the first half of the text in the way it

2. _____ problems such as 'climate disaster' while also offering the 3. _____.

The author 4. _____ the two pathways numerically and employs 5. '_____'

not only to link eating meat with harm to the planet but also to 6. _____ the benefits of

adopting a plant-based diet. The second half of the text is more 7. _____ as the author

details the positives of her firm's products and 8. _____ why they are currently so

expensive. The 9. _____ is effective because she again presents a 10. _____,

i.e. her company is too small, and 11. _____ to the reader to be the solution and help her

company to grow.

5 Tone: The tone of a text can change. Choose six adjectives from the box and write them in the column beside the text to best describe the tone of that part of the text.

> aggressive • critical • humorous • ironic • light-hearted • optimistic • sarcastic • sentimental • serious • urgent • warm-hearted • warning • witty

INCREDIBLE FOODS

Dear Friends, Customers, Investors, Sceptics and Strangers,

If you don't know us that well, you may think Incredible Foods is one of the many companies offering alternatives to meat. Yes, that's what we are, but that's not *all* we are. Our true mission is an ambitious yet realistic strategy to reverse humanity's dangerous course, to turn this beautiful
5 blue, white and green ship around and away from the brink of climate disaster. Imagine we could click our fingers and wish the animal-based food industry away. What would happen? We'd open two completely natural pathways out of the climate crisis. I'm not kidding, folks.

These pathways are:
1. Reduction in methane: Yes, fewer cow farts. Half of the methane added by human activity to the
10 atmosphere comes from the animals we farm for food. The combined climate cost of all that gas is equal to ten years' worth of greenhouse gas emissions at 2020 rates. Although methane is a powerful greenhouse gas, it is different to carbon dioxide in that methane dissipates naturally – it has a half-life of nine years. That means that within nine years of clicking our fingers, half of the methane generated by livestock would've decayed. That's like turning the climate change dooms-
15 day clock back five years!

2. Biomass regrowth: Scientists talk about new technological ways of capturing carbon dioxide from our atmosphere, but they're ignoring Mother Nature's way: photosynthesis, the original carbon-capture technology, perfected through 3 billion years of evolution. Right now, agriculture exploits 45% of the planet's ice-free land, controlling and restricting the growth of green plants
20 and biomass. By clicking our fingers, we would set off an explosion of wild, wonderful green! Top experts estimate regrowth of biomass would suck 800 thousand billion tons of CO_2 from the air and lock it away, undoing 16 years of climate change harm.

Over twenty years, these two natural effects alone would lead to an overall reduction in greenhouse gases. And they're not the only benefits. By farming animals for meat, we are like the
25 asteroid that wiped out the dinosaurs – also alpha predators like us – because it is the top driver of another existential threat to humanity and earth: biodiversity collapse through extinctions, intensive farming and overfishing.

You and I know that it's not as easy as clicking our fingers, but Incredible Foods is here to give humanity a helping hand. It's not magic – it's technology: a novel platform for replacing animal-
30 based meat, dairy and fish with delicious and nutritious foods based on plants. But that's not enough, we need to satisfy meat, fish and dairy lovers, so our products have the appearance, taste and texture of the foods they adore – we know that because they've told us! All the positives and none of the negatives. Who can argue with a win-win proposition like that?

But serious challenges remain. Our products are too expensive, you say, and you're right. Our
35 production costs are high because we're small right now. That's why we urgently need your support to grow so that we can reduce our prices to a level everyone can afford. If you're already convinced, please click on the link at the top of the page to help.
Supporter or sceptic, please let's keep communicating.

Nora Gaffney, CEO Incredible Foods   (561 words)

1 _____
2 _____

3 _____

4 _____

5 _____

6 _____

7 _____

6 In your exercise book, analyse the means the author uses to try to convince her readers of her position. Refer to language and structure.

Writing workshop 2

Do after Section C

Robots and artificial intelligence

On these pages you will work on a creative writing task, namely, a blog post.

1   Not all creative writing text types have the same features.
Look at the box. Informal vocabulary and style are features of a blog post. Circle five more features you would normally find in a blog post.

Look at your student's book pages 126–128 and the PagePlayer App for more help.

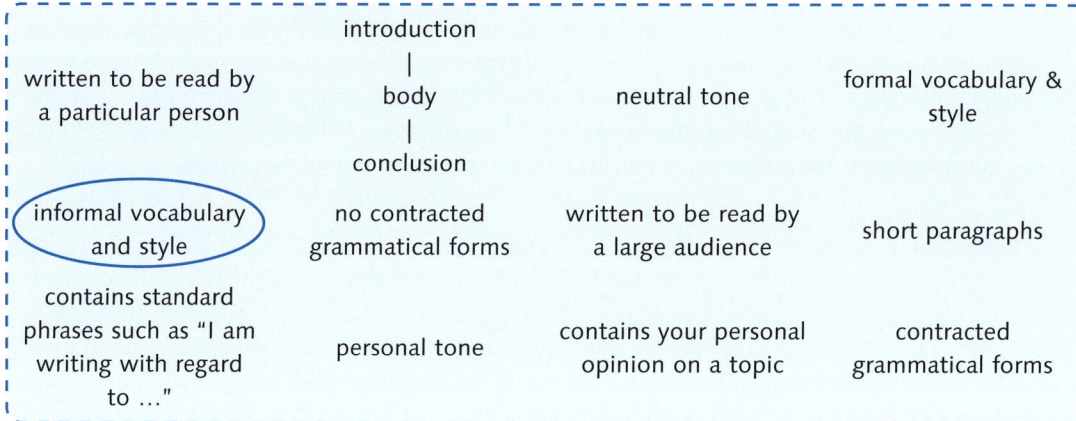

introduction
|
body
|
conclusion

written to be read by a particular person

neutral tone

formal vocabulary & style

informal vocabulary and style

no contracted grammatical forms

written to be read by a large audience

short paragraphs

contains standard phrases such as "I am writing with regard to …"

personal tone

contains your personal opinion on a topic

contracted grammatical forms

2   Connectives are very useful for linking your ideas in a logical way. However, if you are writing in an informal style and you use a formal connective, it can sound wrong. Write the more informal connectives from the box into the table beside the formal connective with the same meaning.

all in all • anyway • ~~as long as~~ • as well as that • but • on top of that • so • that's why

Formal	Informal	Formal	Informal
provided that	*as long as*	in addition to that	
however		moreover	
nevertheless		in conclusion	
consequently		therefore	

3   Read the task and quotation in exercise 6, then answer these questions you should always ask yourself before beginning a creative writing task.

What **perspective** am I writing from?

_____

What is the **purpose** of my text?

_____

Who will read my text (**audience**)?

_____

4   Use the flowchart to brainstorm ideas for your blog. Your work on pages 60–63 of your student's book can help you.

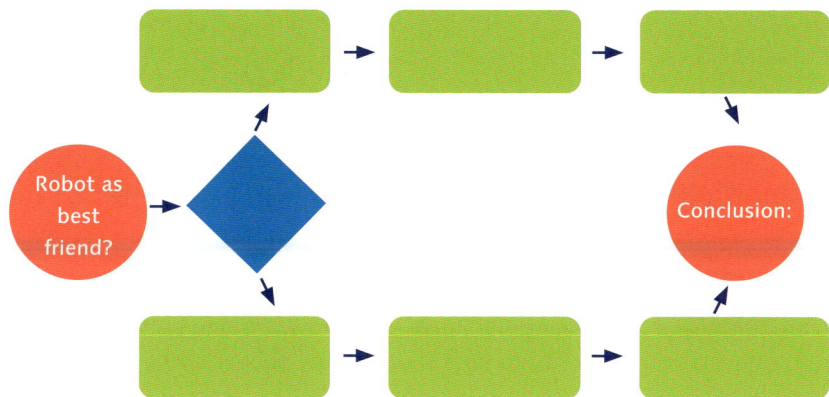

How to write or say it

Informal phrases
Do you ever wonder …?
You must be wondering …
Here's the interesting part …
I know that's a lot to take in, but …
I'm sure you're with me on this one …
There's just one problem …
As if that's not enough …
And on top of that, …
Here's the bottom line …
It all boils down to this …

5   Now create a rough outline of your text in the table below.

Introduction/Opening
Connector
Main body of your text
Conclusion/Closing

6   Now that you have prepared, do the creative writing task in your exercise book.
Your school is holding a week of special events focused on the future. For its website it asks for blog posts on the theme of "Could a robot ever be a BFF?". Write a blog post giving your views. You can refer to the quotation below and the work you have done in class.

"AI programs that say they are listening, pretend they are your friend … But people need relationships, people need people. We can write programs that mimic us, but I don't want to talk to a robot, something without a body, that isn't a child, that didn't have a mother."
Sherry Turkle, science and technology writer and academic

Dealing with listening tasks

Look at your student's book pages 123–125 and the PagePlayer App for more help.

Do after Section A

Genetically modified food

Task type: Matching – multiple choice

In this type of task, you have to choose one correct answer from three possible answers.

1 During your preparation time it can help to brainstorm key words and ideas about the topic. Brainstorm some key vocabulary and ideas using the mind map below. As you write the words, say them in your head. Doing that can help you to hear them if they appear in the audio.

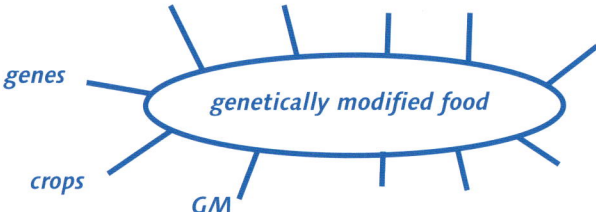

2 Now read the questions in exercise 3 very carefully. Listening to the audio will not help if you do not understand the choices. The audio recording will often contain synonyms of the key words in the questions. Find synonyms for these words taken from the questions.

controversial		sensationalist	
dangers		to accelerate	
rules		to breed	
25 years		drought	

3 Now do the listening task.

You will hear an interview with Linda Shannon, a leading food scientist.
While listening, tick the correct answer. There is only one correct answer.

1 GM food has recently become more controversial because …
- ☐ the government says the risks are exaggerated.
- ☐ the government has relaxed the rules around it.
- ☐ the government has made the rules around it stricter.

2 Linda gives the genetically modified potato as an example of …
- ☐ a GM food that is proven to be safe.
- ☐ a GM food considered risky in 71 countries.
- ☐ the most popular GM food in the last twenty-five years.

3 Linda believes social media and tabloid newspapers …
- ☐ have a role in informing people about GMOs.
- ☐ destroy people's trust in science with sensationalist stories.
- ☐ distract people from serious issues like GM food and health issues.

4 Now is the time to accelerate research into GM food because …
- ☐ breeding new crops in the traditional way is too slow.
- ☐ the government doesn't have time to address everyone's fears.
- ☐ there isn't enough time to trial every drought-resistant GM crop.

5 Global heating, crop-eating insects and diseases mean that …
- ☐ food safety is an urgent issue for everyone everywhere.
- ☐ food safety is not an urgent issue for everyone everywhere.
- ☐ food security is definitely an urgent issue for everyone everywhere.

Words in context

1   Read the text about the problem of deepfakes. Then do exercises 2–4.

Deepfake technology is here to stay and we are to blame

The eerie threat of deepfake technology seems to have come upon us suddenly and taken us unawares. But we shouldn't be surprised. Many of you reading this are too young to remember the analogue days when we used to take photos on film – on 24 or 36-picture rolls! And getting them printed wasn't cheap. Can you **imagine**? You just had one or two chances to capture that
5   memory, and you had to wait a week or two to see if the photo turned out all right. How quaint it all seems now.

Nowadays, our phones are full to the brim not only with thousands of photos, but also hours upon hours of video footage. All seemingly so important that we dare not delete them. But where to store them all? The tech giants have a helpful cloud of course! And how to sort them all? Why our
10   cloud storage **providers** have thought of that too: a kind and helpful AI that will use its facial recognition technology to label the faces of our nearest and dearest. How thoughtful!

Think of it. Millions – no, *billions* of faces for the supercomputers to analyse. Billions of faces making *trillions* of different facial expressions in *quadrillions* of different poses, at different angles and under different lighting conditions. Hours too many to count of home videos, *with audio don't*
15   *forget*, capturing our mannerisms and voices as we live our mundane lives, as well as the moments of joy and surprise, or, as you'll readily find on social media, moments of pain, terror and even death as rubberneckers whip out their smartphones – rather than run for their lives – when caught up in terrible accidents, natural disasters or terror attacks. What's more, if you're a parent like me, you'll have uploaded your children's baby and birthday photos, so the supercomputers
20   can learn how the human face expresses emotion, as well as how our faces develop as we age.

All of that raw data is shared freely with the tech companies, then analysed and processed by unimaginably powerful computers. Our lives are digitized, **broken down into** binary and transformed into code. From this code, amazing algorithms are generated, with the ability to render fake images and video which mimic us so uncannily and so realistically they can fool our primitive eyes and ears.
25   It's all very well to bemoan how we cannot trust what we see in this **digital** age, how trust is being eroded and how our **privacy** is being **infringed**, but how can we complain when we've been feeding the tech giants with our data since the dawn of the internet! The deepfake genie is out of the bottle and we have to live with it. How? First of all, don't be in such a hurry to believe everything you see at first glance – and *don't* share something you suspect or know is fake. Train yourself to check
30   the source of visual material, however genuine it appears, be wary of disinformation and act responsibly: report suspicious material to the platform you found it on.   (522 words)

---

to **be to blame** *schuldig sein*

eerie *unheimlich*

threat *Bedrohung*

to **take sb unawares** *jdn überraschen*

to **capture** *fangen*

to **turn out well/ badly** *gut/schlecht gelingen*

quaint *altmodisch*

brim *Rand*

seemingly *anscheinend*

provider *Anbieter*

facial recognition *Gesichtserkennung*

to **label** *benennen*

thoughtful *rücksichtsvoll*

mannerism *Eigenheit*

mundane *alltäglich*

readily *leicht*

rubbernecker *Gaffer/in, Schaulustige/r*

to **whip out sth** *etw schnell herausziehen*

what's more *darüber hinaus*

raw *(hier) unverarbeitet*

processed *verarbeitet*

unimaginably *unvorstellbar*

digitized *digitalisiert*

to **break sth down into sth** *etw auf etw herunterbrechen*

binary (code) *Binärcode*

to **mimic sb** *jdn nachahmen*

uncannily *unheimlich*

to **fool sb** *jdn täuschen*

to **bemoan sth** *etw lamentieren*

to **erode sth** *etw untergraben*

to **infringe sb's rights** *jds Rechte verletzen*

the dawn of sth *der Beginn von etw*

genie (in a bottle) *Flaschengeist, Dschinn*

however *ganz egal wie*

genuine *echt*

wary *vorsichtig*

to **report sth/sb** *etw/jdn melden*

suspicious *verdächtig*

2   You can find the highlighted words from the text on page 25 in the table below. Fill in the empty boxes in the following wordlist.

Word/Phrase	Memory support	German
_____ _____	**SENTENCE:** If a task seems complicated, it can help to _____ it _____ smaller steps.	etw auf etw herunterbrechen
digital	**WORD FAMILY** _____ (vb) _____ (n) _____ (adj) digital (adj) _____ (adv)	digital
imagine	**WORD FAMILY** to imagine (vb) _____ (n) _____ (adj) (un-) _____ (adj) (un-) _____ (adj) _____ (adv)	sich vorstellen
_____	**COLLOCATIONS** to ~ (on) sb's rights, privacy, territory to ~ a law, a rule, a contract, a trademark	verletzen, verstoßen
_____	**COLLOCATIONS** absolute / complete / total ~ to ensure / to guarantee / to safeguard (sb's) ~ an intrusion of (sb's) ~ / an invasion of (sb's) ~ in ~ in the ~ of (e.g. your home/bedroom/office)	Privatsphäre
_____	**COLLOCATIONS** internet / cable TV / mobile phone / service ~,	Anbieter

3   Pronounce these words from 'Words in context', writing down the correct spelling.

[ˌrekəgˈnɪʃn]   _____   [ɪˈmaʊʃn]   _____

[ˈdɪdʒɪtl]   _____   [ˈdʒenjuɪn]   _____

[ɪˈraʊd]   _____   [ˈɔːdiəʊ]   _____

4   Complete the sentences with words from 'Words in context'. You are given the first letter and the lines tell you how many letters are in the word.

1 Before sharing photos, you should use the tools today's smartphones have to remove identifying and location *d* __ __ __ from them.

2 The challenge posed by deepfake photos and videos is that it is getting more and more difficult to know whether they are *g* __ __ __ __ __ __ or fake.

3 Everyone thinks they'll never be *f* __ __ __ __ __ by a deepfake photo or video, but that's arrogant.

4 Don't share deepfakes because if you do, social media *a* __ __ __ __ __ __ __ __ __ will push them higher in people's feeds.

5 If you don't like *f* __ __ __ __ __ __ __ __ __ __ __ __ __ __ __ __, you should check the privacy settings in your cloud storage and in your social media accounts – you can make sure it is turned off.

The chill out zone

1 Strange but true

The descriptions (a-f) describe the origins of six of the eight words in the box. Match them with their description.

TIP: Entering the word and the term 'etymology' in a search engine can help.

byte	bug	code	computer	googol	hacker	nerd	spam

a This word originally meant cheap tinned meat. Today, however, it refers to numerous, unwanted messages sent over the internet. This modern meaning seems to come from a 1970s comedy sketch by Monty Python where a café's menu has many options, but all are the tinned meat.

_____

b This is the number 1 followed by 100 zeroes and was the original name of a famous search engine. It was chosen as a joke at first about how much information the engine could search.

_____

c This word first appeared in print in a book for children by Dr Seuss in 1950. It was an imaginary character, who isn't described in detail. It may also come from the 1940s American slang word for a stupid or crazy person, which itself originally came from 'nut'.

_____

d This word seems to come from an old word for somebody who did a simple, routine job. In the 1970s, it became used to describe somebody who liked to experiment with IT and programming, sometimes creatively, sometimes foolishly. In the eighties, its meaning changed again to describe somebody who accesses computer systems illegally.

_____

e This word was used for a long time to refer to faults or problems with mechanical devices. In 1947, however, Grace Hopper, an American computer scientist working at Harvard University, discovered an insect – a moth – inside a broken computer. She removed it, the computer worked again and she noted it as a computer '_____'. The insect can still be seen in the Smithsonian Museum today.

_____

f This was first used to describe people who performed mathematical calculations mentally and then later with the help of calculators. It was with the help of women in this role, mainly black women, that NASA's space programme was so successful in the 1950s and 60s.

_____

2 Word search

Find the six English words in the word search and write them under their German equivalent.

Betrüger

_____

Film-/Bildmaterial

_____

Gerät, technischer Krimskrams

_____

Haushaltsgerät

_____

Überwachung

_____

Widerstand

_____

J	R	E	S	I	S	T	A	N	C	E
J	K	S	U	Y	K	O	N	O	A	V
F	L	F	R	A	U	D	S	T	E	R
O	Y	Q	V	M	X	W	Q	T	L	C
O	X	H	E	R	B	I	C	I	D	E
T	M	X	I	R	G	V	Y	S	F	W
A	P	P	L	I	A	N	C	E	K	W
G	Y	X	L	M	X	L	P	H	R	G
E	L	B	A	N	H	S	J	O	I	A
M	V	T	N	Q	G	P	K	W	M	D
A	R	O	C	P	T	I	D	K	N	G
A	S	R	E	P	L	I	C	A	T	E
Y	A	K	B	M	T	Q	W	X	Q	T

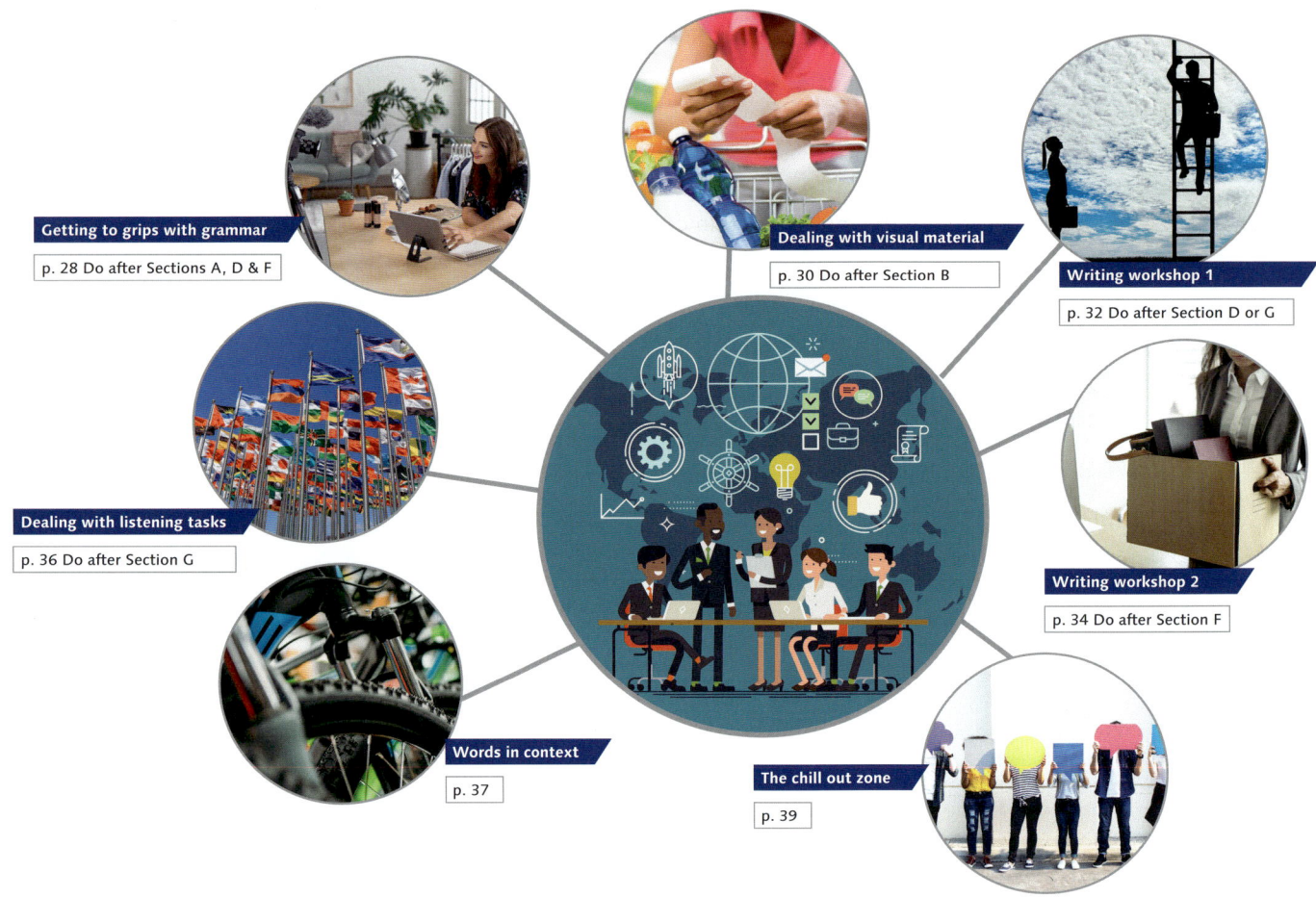

Getting to grips with grammar
p. 28 Do after Sections A, D & F

Dealing with visual material
p. 30 Do after Section B

Writing workshop 1
p. 32 Do after Section D or G

Writing workshop 2
p. 34 Do after Section F

Dealing with listening tasks
p. 36 Do after Section G

Words in context
p. 37

The chill out zone
p. 39

Getting to grips with grammar

G ▶ *Defining and non-defining relative clauses, SB, p. 295*

Do after Section A

1 Defining and non-defining relative clauses

Rewrite the sentences in your exercise book. Use a defining or non-defining relative clause to include the information in brackets.

1 In most countries, social media posts must be labelled with #Ad or #Paid.
(The posts advertise brands and products.)

2 However, influencers can share their opinions about products and brands without these hashtags.
(They actually use the products and brands.)

3 This raises the question: how can <u>we</u> tell if a post is a genuine product review or a paid-for ad?
(Product reviews do not need the #Ad label.)

4 Last September, the UK Advertising Standards Agency checked 122 Instagram influencer accounts and all their posts.
(The posts were uploaded over a three-week period.)

5 The check revealed that only 35% of paid-for advertising posts were correctly labelled as adverts.
(The check involved looking at 24,000 posts.)

6 The agency did not name the people but is thinking about naming-and-shaming them in the future.
(The people broke the rules.)

Do after Section D

G ▸ *Reported speech, SB, p.288*

2 Reported speech

Write the direct speech as reported speech. The first one has been done for you.

1 Woman: "Will I earn less if I work from home?"

The woman asked / wanted to know if/whether she would earn less if she worked from home.

2 Manager → employees: "Please use the mute button in online meetings when you aren't speaking."

_____

3 Colleague → female colleague: "Report our boss because he is discriminating against you."

_____

4 Workers → management: "Can the company provide more childcare places for our children?"

_____

5 Business expert → audience: "Do not expect equality to be achieved overnight."

_____

6 Journalist: "How long will it be until all workers have the right to flexible working?"

_____

7 Father → child: "Don't disturb me now – I'm working."

_____

Do after Section F

G ▸ *Adjectives and adverbs, SB, p.293*

3 Adjectives and adverbs

There are two adjectives in brackets after the statements below. Complete the statements in your exercise book by using one adjective and putting the other one in its adverb form.

1 The universal basic income may have worked _____ in Finland, but Finnish society is _____ to British society and we cannot expect UBI to work in Britain. **(different, good)**

2 A guaranteed income will send the message that you do not have to work _____ to succeed in life because the government will take care of you. Do we want a society of _____ people? **(hard, lazy)**

3 The universal basic income is set at a _____ level. So I think critics are _____ overreacting – unemployed people will still want to find a job that pays more. **(complete, low)**

4 A universal income is the _____ answer to unemployment because it ignores the fact that some people have financial supports that poor people do not. Society's limited resources must be distributed _____. **(fair, wrong)**

5 The scheme in Finland seems _____ when you consider the results. Yes, it reduced insecurity and stress for some, but only a few more people receiving the UBI _____ found jobs than the group who didn't receive it. **(expensive, successful)**

Dealing with visual material

Do after Section B

1 Match the sentence beginnings (1–5) with the correct ending (a–f) to make possible interpretations of the cartoon. There is one ending you do not need.

1 The cartoon implies that only the wealthy can afford …

2 I believe the cartoonist conveys a rather mixed message because …

3 What surprises me is that due to her rude and arrogant comment, the wealthy lady does not …

4 Although the poor lady is clearly meant to be a consumer of cheap fashion, her appearance does not …

5 It can be concluded that the cartoon is saying that ethical consumption is an option which …

a … Crymark is obviously a play on the name of a well-known European fast fashion retailer.

b … to consider things like ethics when buying clothes.

c … seem like the kind of person who would care how or where her clothes are made.

d … both characters are depicted in a negative light.

e … is available only to the rich.

f … seem to be fashionable in any way.

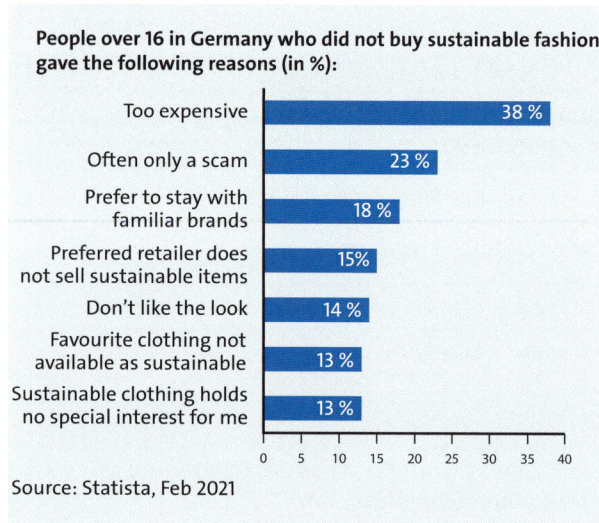

People over 16 in Germany who did not buy sustainable fashion gave the following reasons (in %):

Source: Statista, Feb 2021

2 Look at the information in the graph on the left. Now decide if the interpretations (1–5) are based on information in the graph or not. Label them 'correct' if they are, or 'incorrect' if they are not.

1 It could be argued that an easy way to increase the amount of sustainable fashion would be to make it more available because between 13 to 18% said their favourite shops or brands don't have sustainable options.

_____

2 Almost a quarter of people have bought fashion that was labelled sustainable, but it actually wasn't.

_____

3 The graph shows that four out of ten people believe that brands are unfairly charging more for the sustainable label.

_____

4 A significant minority say that the higher price of sustainable fashion stops them buying it.

_____

5 I conclude from the graph that there is an issue of trust for some consumers – nearly a quarter of the people surveyed don't buy sustainable fashion because they say it's often a scam.

_____

3 In a sequence 2 oral communication exam task, keep in mind that it is not a competition between you and your speaking partner. If you disagree with your partner, explain why politely and give them a chance to accept your opinion or move the discussion along. If you agree with your partner, give a reason or add a supporting point. Above all, be fair to each other and give each other equal chances to speak.

Label each of the phrases below according to what they express as in the example.
TIP: It is very helpful to memorize standard phrases such as these.

A agreement *(Zustimmung)* **B clarification** *(Abklärung)* **C disagreement** *(Uneinigkeit)*

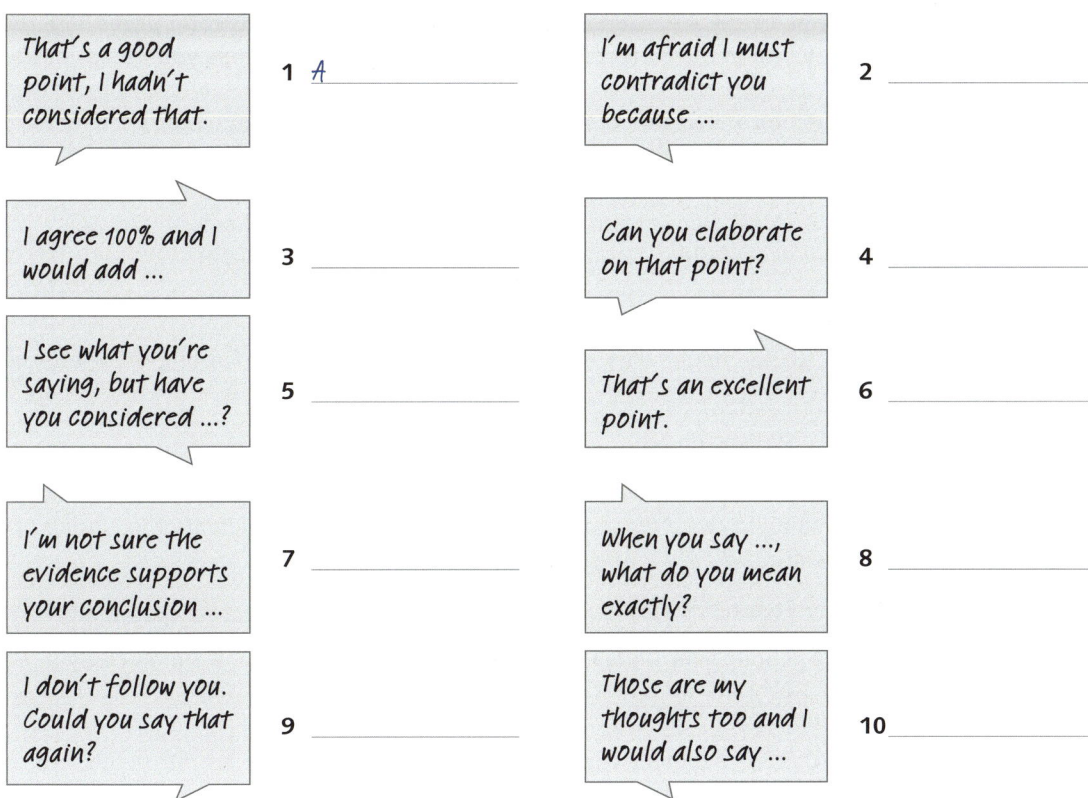

That's a good point, I hadn't considered that.	**1** _A_____
I'm afraid I must contradict you because ...	**2** _____
I agree 100% and I would add ...	**3** _____
Can you elaborate on that point?	**4** _____
I see what you're saying, but have you considered ...?	**5** _____
That's an excellent point.	**6** _____
I'm not sure the evidence supports your conclusion ...	**7** _____
When you say ..., what do you mean exactly?	**8** _____
I don't follow you. Could you say that again?	**9** _____
Those are my thoughts too and I would also say ...	**10** _____

4 In a sequence 2 task, you are asked to discuss the following statement:

Ethical consumption is impossible in our society.

Using phrases from exercise 3 and your own ideas, write down in your exercise book what you could say if your partner made the statements below. You can use information from the visual material on the previous page and from the text on ethical consumption on pages 96–97 in your student's book.

1 "I agree with the statement because you can see in the graph that nearly 40% of people can't afford sustainable fashion."

2 "The statement is correct and so is the author of the text – you can never be sure that what you buy is ethical. So there's no point feeling bad about it."

3 "I don't think the statement is right. We can buy ethical goods if we choose carefully. And as the author of the text says, if we find sustainable goods, we should tell our friends so they can buy them too."

4 "In my opinion, the statement is too extreme. The article and the cartoon don't mention the most important fact: that we buy too many things that we don't need. The most ethical thing to do is buy less stuff."

Writing workshop 1

Do after Sections D or G

Look at your student's book pages 213–218 and the PagePlayer App for more help.

1 When analysing a text in an exam, a common task is to analyse how the author of a text achieves his/her aim. This involves examining the style, language and techniques used, their effects on the reader and how these can help the writer to achieve his or her aim, e.g. convince the reader to agree, persuade the reader of the need for action / the urgency of a situation.

The quotes and features below are taken from the 'Cultural Complexity' text on pages 114–116 of your student's book. Write in the correct label from the box. There are three you do not need.

> call to action • repetition • engaging opening • strong, determined language • personification • informal register • expert opinion • directly addressing the reader

1 "it could cost you the deal you've been working on" (l. 8), "overseas clients will be as unprepared for your way of doing business as you are for theirs" (ll. 51–52)

   Technique / Stylistic device: _____

2 "cultural cock-ups" (l. 4), "flummoxed" (l. 46), "dipped his toe" (l. 62) "cutting them a lot of slack" (l. 80),

   Technique / Stylistic device: _____

3 "It's mid-afternoon in downtown Ulaanbaatar, Mongolia. Five or six guests are sat around a restaurant table waiting to share fermented mare's milk with you to celebrate the closing of an important business deal." (ll. 1–3)

   Technique / Stylistic device: _____

4 Successful business people: Will Tindall, (ll. 4–5) Louis Barnett, (l. 42) and Simon Duffy (l. 61)

   Technique / Stylistic device: _____

5 "incredibly badly" (l. 28), "definitely frowned upon" (l. 29), "a valuable lesson" (l. 32), "incredibly important" (l. 33), "it is crucial" (l. 52), "you have to be prepared" (ll. 77–78)

   Technique / Stylistic device: _____

2 Choose two of the five devices from exercise 1. Read the text on pages 114–116 of your student's book again and then say how they help the author to convince readers of his/her view that 'doing your homework' is vital when doing business with people from other cultures. An example has been done for you. Write your answers in your exercise book.

Technique / Stylistic device: *informal register*

The author wants to convince businesspeople in general and not just experts, so he / she uses an informal register with expressions such as 'cultural cock-ups' (l. 4) and 'flummoxed' (l. 46). Furthermore, idiomatic phrases such as 'dipped his toe' (l. 62) and 'cutting them a lot of slack' (l. 81) give the text a more relaxed tone so that the reader does not feel they are being told what to do.

3 Here is another text for you to analyse. First, read it and decide where in the text (A–D) four of these headings should go.

1 Higher pay for all improves productivity _____

2 One short question with many negative consequences _____

3 The gender pay gap is bad for women and bad for firms _____

4 A low-cost, simple measure with proven benefits _____

5 Asking about salary history is fair _____

6 Making the change can improve your firm's reputation _____

How one simple change could solve the gender pay gap

By Jemima Olchawski

[...] Progress to close the UK's pernicious gender pay gap has been slow and if things don't speed up, we won't see it done until 2050.

A

[The gender pay gap is] damaging to the women who will spend their entire working lives earning below their potential and then go on to retire with smaller pensions. But it also means businesses are missing out. There's good evidence that gender equality in the workplace improves performance and productivity. More needs to be done and the good news is that there's a simple yet effective step that employers can take right now to narrow their pay gaps – they just need to stop asking potential employees about their salary history. [...]

B

It's an easy step with no big costs attached and there's compelling evidence to suggest it has helped to narrow pay gaps – not only for women but for people of colour and people with disabilities, too. Effects have ranged from closing 4.7 per cent of the existing gender pay gap for all employees to a 6.2 per cent boost to women's pay, which closes 43 per cent of the gender pay gap (and half of racial pay gaps) for job-changers. [...]

C

Like many others, I know how it feels to be asked about my salary when I've been applying for a job – it's uncomfortable and it's unfair. Our answers are most often used to determine pay offers although some employers say that they're used for 'benchmarking'.

The question might not seem significant, but it absolutely is. What many employers don't realise is that by asking for salary history, they are perpetuating the gender pay gap. Women tend to earn less and so sharing this information can encourage employers to make a lower offer than they might otherwise and it doesn't just impact women. It also bakes in race and disability inequality in the workplace. By basing a salary offer on salary history an employer may unintentionally take on pay gaps started in other organisations.

D

Ending salary history would benefit everyone, not just women. Fifty-eight per cent of men say that they would think more highly of an employer who chose not to ask salary history questions and 63 per cent of women agreed. [...] Sixty-one per cent of women who have been asked about salary history say it damaged their confidence to negotiate for better pay.

Not asking salary history questions makes the bargaining process fairer, improves employers' reputation with employees and can help improve gender equality within an organisation. It's a win-win.

(489 words)   Source: *The Telegraph*, 18 November 2021

4 Analyse the techniques and stylistic devices the author uses to convince employers that by not asking job candidates about their salary history they can help reduce the gender pay gap.

Writing workshop 2

Do after Section F

1   Write the following phrases from speeches into the correct stage.

Look at your student's book pages 126–128 and the PagePlayer App for more help.

First, we need to ask ourselves … • Let me close by asking you all a question … • My topic today is … • In conclusion, … • First, I will address … and then … followed by … • Now I will turn to … • I would like to speak to you about … • When you consider the arguments I have made, I am sure you will agree that … • We must also take into account that … • The next point I would like to look at is …

Introduction

a _____

b _____

c _____

Main part

d _____

e _____

f _____

g _____

Closing

h _____

i _____

j _____

2   It can be very helpful to learn phrases that you can use when giving a speech or writing a comment to express how sure you are in your knowledge and opinions.
Label each of the phrases, as in the example, according to what they convey:

A a certainty *(Sicherheit)*, **B** an assumption *(Vermutung)*, **C** a doubt *(Zweifel)*

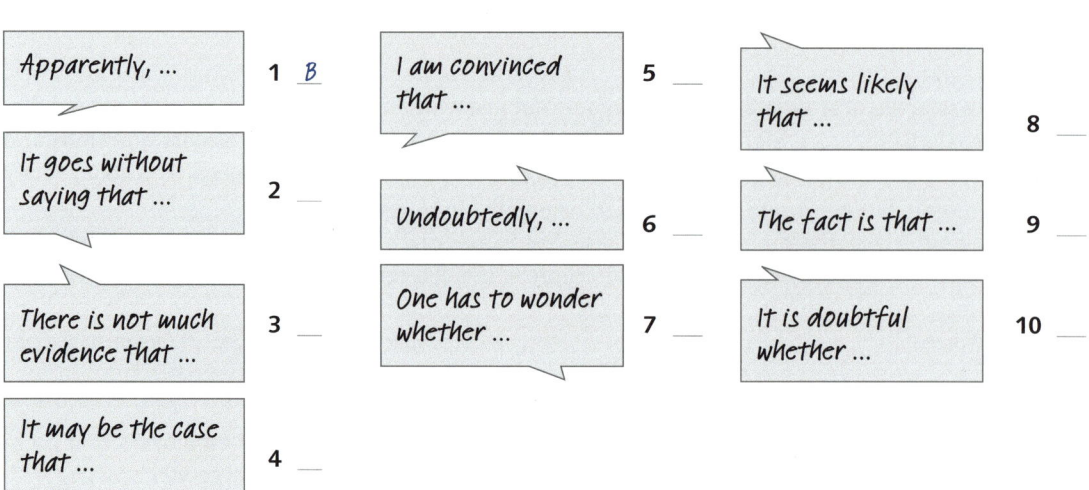

Apparently, …   **1** _B_

It goes without saying that …   **2** __

There is not much evidence that …   **3** __

It may be the case that …   **4** __

I am convinced that …   **5** __

Undoubtedly, …   **6** __

One has to wonder whether …   **7** __

It seems likely that …   **8** __

The fact is that …   **9** __

It is doubtful whether …   **10** __

3 a You are taking part in a conference on youth unemployment. Write a speech in which you appeal to the audience to support the introduction of a universal basic income in your country.
Look at the rough plan of a speech (1–6) below. Match six of the eight bullet points (a–h) to the correct part of the outline. The first one has been done for you.

Speech plan

1 Introduction __h__

2 Outline ____

3 Description of UBI ____

4 Criticisms ____

5 Rebuttal of criticisms ____

6 Conclusion ____

a summary of my opinion & call to action → agree with me!! ☺

b doesn't make unemployment worse, saves money on crime & bad mental health, reduces costs of current social security system

c signpost for my audience:
1st → UBI description
2nd → criticisms
3rd → benefits → closing

d what UBI means esp. 'universal' & what it is

e how social security works in Germany – ALG I and ALG II (Hartz IV)

f raise taxes on the wealthy and offer uni places to every unemployed person!!

g discourages people from finding jobs, too expensive & not fair to give money to the rich

h nice to be here & introduce the topic

3 b Now write your own speech to the youth conference. Use the structure from exercise 1 and some phrases from exercises 1 and 2.
You may use the ideas from exercise 3a) or your own ideas. Your work on pages 110–113 of your student's book will be useful.

How to say it or write it				
Introducing yourself	**Introducing the topic**	**Stating your aims**	**Linking ideas**	**Ending the speech**
Hello everybody and welcome … I'm … / My name's … from … (organization). It's nice to see so many people here today.	I'm here to talk to you about … / I'd like to talk to you about … The reason I'm here today is to … / I'm here today to tell you about …	First, I'd like to tell you about … Then … I'd like to start by explaining / introducing / outlining … I'd like to take this opportunity to tell you / say a few words about …	Let's move on to … / Let me turn to … Another important aspect is …	To sum up, … Thank you all for listening / for your time. Does anyone have a question? / Any questions?

35

Dealing with listening tasks

Look at your student's book pages 123–125 and the PagePlayer App for more help.

Do after Section G

Intercultural competence in the workplace

Task type: short answers

In this type of task, you are often given some short points and must listen for those that are missing.
This missing information must be summarized in short, grammatically correct sentences.
The sentences you are given will usually contain some words used in the listening text.
This will help you concentrate on the answers you need during your first listen.

🔊 03 **1** You are going to listen to an intercultural competence trainer and a critic give their views on the training.
Before you listen, read the task and activate your previous knowledge by brainstorming ideas.
Write short answers for the two missing points in both a) and b).

a Give reasons why the trainer feels intercultural training is necessary.

- People in the West assume everyone now accepts Western culture.

– _____

- The Western way of doing business has not become the norm.

– _____

b State arguments which the critic makes against intercultural competence training.

- The trainers are not really experts.

– _____

– _____

- Foreign business partners will have done their own research, so small misunderstandings won't stand in the way of doing business.

🔊 04 **2** You are going to listen to two participants in an intercultural awareness training course give their opinions of the training. Write short answers for the two missing points in both a) and b).

a List the positive effects the training had.

- It challenged people's assumptions.

– _____

– _____

- It made people aware of their unconscious negative bias.

b State the criticisms made of the training.

- It focused too much on doing business abroad.

– _____

- The trainer ignored a complaint about a lack of respect for different cultures.

– _____

Words in context

1 Read the text about British spending on ethical products.

UK annual spending on ethical products surpasses £100bn for first time

Britons' annual spending on ethical products and investments has surpassed £100bn for the first time, as lifestyle changes linked to Covid and the climate crisis stoked demand for plant-based foods, secondhand clothes and furniture, and greener gadgets.

5 The value of the "green" pound surged by nearly a quarter to £122bn in 2020, according to a new Co-op report covering the most recent year for which figures are available. That total was bolstered by £57bn of ethical savings and investments.

Shoppers spent £61bn on ethical products and services, which was nearly 30% more than in 2019. That equates to £2,189 a household, a £489 increase. The equivalent figure for 2010 was £1,028.

10 The retailer's ethical consumerism report, which is a barometer of the extent to which consumers' shopping habits reflect their concerns about the environment, animal welfare and social justice, also found more shoppers were boycotting brands on ethical or social concerns. These businesses suffered a £3.9bn loss of sales, which was £600m bigger than the previous year.

Steve Murrells, the Co-op's chief executive, said shoppers were "turning up the heat" to get
15 companies to change. The boycotts were a "warning to brands that they must do business in a better way for workers, communities and the planet", he said.

The huge increase in ethical spending also showed that when businesses provide choice, and the government offers helpful incentives, "consumers will respond positively", Murrells added.

The area of the market that saw the biggest increase was eco-travel and transport, where sales rose
20 by more than 70% to £12.2bn. This reflected the rise in electric car ownership as well as the impact of the pandemic, which revived cycling to levels last seen in Britain in the 1960s.

Britons are also trying to make their homes greener by investing in energy-efficient boilers as well as other household appliances or switching to "green" electricity deals. Taken together this market had expanded by a third to be worth £20.5bn.

25 However, this push fell short of what is needed to hit the government's net zero targets, the Co-op said. For example, while households spent £5bn on energy-efficient gas boilers, just £130m went on heat pumps.

The report also highlighted the growing appetite to buy secondhand goods, be it for financial or environmental reasons. Sales of secondhand clothes increased by nearly a quarter to £864m
30 while spending on "pre-loved" furniture was up by more than £100m at £837m.

In the now £14bn ethical food and drink market the sales trends reflect people making changes to their diet, with demand for vegetarian and plant-based foods up 34% at £1.5bn. Fairtrade and organic food also grew strongly, up 14% and 13% respectively, while free-range egg sales exceeded £1bn for the first time.

35 (453 words)   Source: *The Guardian*, 31 December 2021

to **surpass** *übersteigen*

annual *jährlich*

to **stoke sth** *etw schüren*

to **surge** *(stark) ansteigen*

to **bolster** *stärken, unterstützen*

savings *Spareinlagen, Ersparnisse*

to **equate to sth** *etw entsprechen*

retailer *Vertreiber/in, Einzelhändler/in*

to **reflect sth** *etw (wieder-) spiegeln*

concern *Sorge*

animal welfare *Tierwohl*

to **suffer sth** *etw erfahren*

eco- (ecological) *umweltfreundlich*

to **revive sb/sth** *jdn/etw wiederbeleben, auffrischen*

household appliance *Haushaltsgerät*

boiler *Heizungskessel*

heat pump *Wärmepumpe*

"pre-loved" *gebraucht*

respectively *jeweils*

to **exceed** *übersteigen*

2 You can find the highlighted words from the text on page 37 in the table below.
Fill in the empty boxes in the following wordlist.

Word/Phrase	Memory support	German
_____	**COLLOCATIONS** ~ identity, awareness, marketing, loyalty fashionable, hot, reputable, sustainable, own ~ to ~ sth (as sth)	Handelsmarke
consumerism	**WORD FAMILY** to _____ (v) consumerism (n) _____ (n) (public/human/domestic) _____ (of sth) (n)	Konsumerismus, Verbraucherherrschaft
demand	**SENTENCE:** _____ _____	Nachfrage
_____	**COLLOCATIONS** ~ consumer, consumption, grounds, products and services, food and drink, savings and investment, spending	ethisch
_____	**SENTENCE:** If we want people to buy more sustainable goods, there should be more _____s to encourage them.	Anreiz
_____	**COLLOCATIONS** ~ food/fruit/vegetables/cheese/wine, etc. produce, farm/er/ing, horticulture	biologisch

3 Pronounce these words from 'Words in context', writing down the correct spelling.

[sɜːʤ] _____   [ɪˈkwɪvələnt] _____

[kənˈsɜːn] _____   [ˈenəʤi ɪˈfɪʃənt] _____

[ˌʧiːfɪgˈzɛkjʊtɪv] _____   [ˌvɛʤɪˈteərɪən] _____

4 Complete the collocations using a word from the box. You may need to change the form of
verbs. There are three words you do not need.

> appetite • bolster • do • make • reflect • stoke • suffer • surpass

1 The annual release of new smartphone models _____ **demand** and keeps tech
companies' profits high.

2 A leading retailer of fast fashion has _____ **losses** for the first time in twenty years.

3 The retailer's poor sales might _____ shoppers' **concerns** about child and
sweatshop labour in clothes making.

4 Consumers should not forget that how they behave can have an influence on the way retailers
_____ **business**.

5 This **growth** has been _____ by government incentives and tax breaks which
reduce e-cars' price tag.

The chill out zone

1 How culturally competent are you?
Read these interesting facts about different cultures. Put a tick (✓) in the correct box.

	True	False
1 In English-speaking cultures, you should not use 'Miss' when speaking to a business woman. It is better to use 'Ms' – it rhymes with 'biz'.	☐	☐
2 In Arab countries, you should stand close to the person you are speaking to – one metre or less.	☐	☐
3 In the US, workers should never call their boss by their first name.	☐	☐
4 In a full restaurant in Spain, you should not try to share a table with strangers.	☐	☐

2 Idioms at work
Connect the idioms to the correct definition. The first has been done for you.
If you are not sure, check in a dictionary.

1 to get the sack	**a** to start work early and finish it late
2 a ballpark figure	**b** a very important person, usually the boss
3 a bean counter	**c** to be dismissed from your job
4 to burn the candle at both ends	**d** to make a living
5 a big cheese	**e** an approximate number
6 to earn a crust	**f** to be very busy
7 to be snowed under	**g** an accountant / a bookkeeper

3 Topic quiz
How well do you know Topic 3 in your student's book? Choose the right answers and the letters should spell what women deserve.

a What percentage of the world's population belonged to Gen Z in 2019?

F 39%   **E** 32%   **G** 29%

b Gleam Futures, an agency for social media stars, prefer which term instead of 'influencers'?

A Genuinfluencers   **R** Talent-first Digital Stars   **Q** Digital-first talent

c In most countries, what percentage of male pay do women receive for the same work?

M 45–60%   **U** 60–75%   **E** 75–90%

d According to the World Bank, what does two-thirds of the world's trade flow through?

A Global supply chains   **E** Airports and sea ports   **S** China

e Which of these is considered a benefit of globalization?

B Exploitation of workers   **H** Tariffs   **L** Lower production costs

f Which of these word pairs is NOT a collocation in English?

C Moral dilemma   **O** Negative impact   **P** Ethical conscious

g The Covid-19 pandemic has led to a dramatic increase in people …

Y Home office.   **A** Working remotely.   **E** Living at work.

h What do 93% of Gen Zers expect from their employer?
Y A positive impact on society   **R** Free smartphones and gadgets   **K** Unlimited holidays

What do women deserve? ___ ___ ___ ___ ___ ___ ___ ___

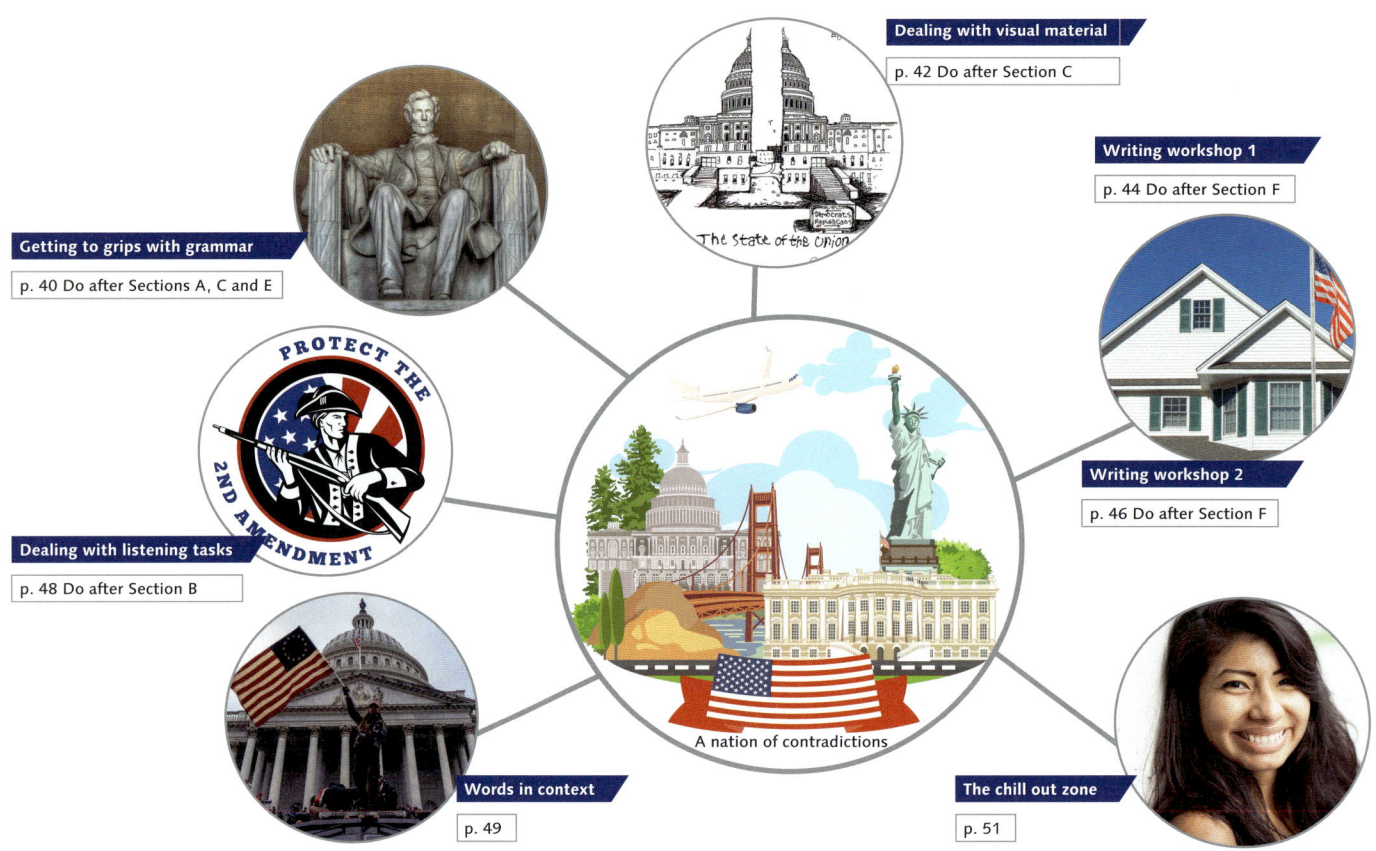

Getting to grips with grammar
p. 40 Do after Sections A, C and E

Dealing with visual material
p. 42 Do after Section C

Writing workshop 1
p. 44 Do after Section F

Writing workshop 2
p. 46 Do after Section F

Dealing with listening tasks
p. 48 Do after Section B

The state of the Union

A nation of contradictions

Words in context
p. 49

The chill out zone
p. 51

Getting to grips with grammar

Do after Section A

G ▸ *Conditionals,*
SB, p. 291

1 Using conditionals

The writer of the text below has made mistakes using conditional forms. Find six conditional sentences and cross out the wrong forms. Then write the sentences out correctly in your exercise book. The first one has been done for you.

The name: If you ~~will~~ ask US citizens, many don't know that America comes from Amerigo Vespucci, an Italian explorer, and that America was first used to describe what is now Brazil.

The flag: The current US flag was designed by Ohio high school student, Robert Heft, as a school assignment. His teacher gave him a B minus grade but told him he would raise the grade if the flag would be accepted as the United States' official flag. It was, so Robert got a better grade.

Geography: The US will look very different today if it hadn't bought land: Florida and Alaska were bought from Spain and Russia, respectively, and the land sold by France in the 1803 Louisiana Purchase includes land that makes up part or all of fifteen present-day federal states.

The people: The US is seen, rightly or wrongly, as a white country but if current population trends continued, the majority of US citizens are non-white in twenty-five years' time.

Ethnicity: Americans with German roots are the largest ancestry group in the US. As a group, they will be half the size of Germany's population if you added them together: 43 million.

Traditions: If there hadn't been so much immigration from Germany throughout its history, the US won't have some of its most loved traditions today: the Christmas tree, kindergartens, hot dogs or hamburgers!

Do after Section C

2 The present perfect vs the simple past

G ▸ *The simple past, SB, p. 284; the present perfect, SB, p. 284*

Complete the sentences by putting the verbs into the correct tense: present perfect or simple past.

1 Alternative political parties _____ (never, be able to) gain as much

support as the Democrats and Republicans.

2 In the last two presidential elections, third party candidates _____

(receive) less than 5% of the votes cast.

3 Older Americans are not divided when it comes to the US flag: in a poll last month, 86% of people

over 55 _____ (say) the flag makes them feel very proud.

4 Since 2016 the percentage of young Americans who feel very proud of their country _____

(fall) from 34% to 20%.

5 Although Americans' views of the BLM movement are polarized, last year three out of four

Americans polled _____ (believe) that non-violent protest could

improve the situation of Black people in the US.

6 A more worrying trend, however, is that support for violent action _____

(grow) by 300% over the last 30 years.

7 A respected opinion polling organization _____ (just, publish) a poll

showing that 40% of Americans do not believe Joe Biden won the 2020 presidential election fairly.

8 This fact makes the challenge which President Biden _____

(describe) in his inauguration speech to "write an American story ... of unity, not division" even

more difficult, if not impossible.

Do after Section E

3 Countable and uncountable nouns

G ▸ *Countable and uncountable nouns, SB, p. 297*

Fill each of the gaps below with two words, as in the example. Put the nouns in the plural form where possible.

1 *Some people* believe America has been involved in too _____ - when has there

been _____, they ask.

> any, many, ~~some~~ • peace, ~~person~~, war

2 There was _____ that America's standing in the world would improve after

Biden's election, but opinion polls so far haven't shown _____

of _____.

> an, any, some • evidence, hope, improvement

3 Despite _____, such as the US rejoining the Paris climate agreement, many

experts say that _____ needs to be done if we are to limit _____

to our planet from climate change.

> a lot of, some, the • damage, progress, work

Dealing with visual material

Do after Section C

1 Read the quotation below. Now say where it comes from and summarize it in one sentence.

"Let us listen to one another.
Hear one another.
See one another.
Show respect to one another.
Politics need not be a raging fire destroying everything in its path.
Every disagreement doesn't have to be a cause for total war."

President Biden, Inaugural Address, Jan 20th, 2021

_____

_____

_____

_____

_____

_____

How to say it or write it
The quotation is taken from …   The remarks were made in …   It is a plea for …   Biden is urging the …   He believes that …

Look at your student's book pages 43–44 and the PagePlayer App for more help.

2 Describe the bar chart below and explain the trend it shows.

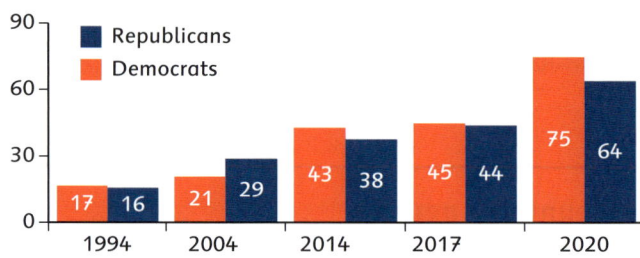

% SHARE OF REPUBLICANS AND DEMOCRATS WHO
HAVE A VERY NEGATIVE VIEW OF THE OPPOSING PARTY

■ Republicans
■ Democrats

	1994	2004	2014	2017	2020
Democrats	17	21	43	45	75
Republicans	16	29	38	44	64

Sources: Statista 2022; The Survey Center on American Life 2020

_____

_____

_____

_____

_____

_____

_____

How to say it or write it
The bar chart shows …   The chart is based on two sources of data, namely, … and …   The horizontal axis / x-axis shows the years …   There is a clear upward trend …   Between … and …, there was a steady / significant increase in …

3 Complete the description of the cartoon with the correct words from the box.

background | caption | corner | depicts | divided | foreground |
halves | separated | sign | tone

The black and white cartoon 1. _____ the

Capitol Building in Washington, D.C. The building, however,

is 2. _____ into two

3. _____ which are

4. _____ by an empty space.

Through this space, one can see other buildings in the

5. _____ and even some birds

flying in the sky. Each half of the Capitol has its own steps leading

to a doorway. There are more steps leading up to the door on the right half of the picture than on

the left. A 6. _____ in the lower right-hand

7. _____ in the 8. _____ has

two arrows and the words "Democrats" and "Republicans". The arrow for the Democrats points

towards the left half of the Capitol, while the Republican arrow points to the right half.

The 9. _____ at the bottom of the cartoon says "The State of

the Union". The black and white colour of the cartoon gives it a serious

10. _____ .

> **Look at your student's book pages 82–83 and the PagePlayer App for more help.**

4 Interpret the message of the cartoon considering also what you learned from the bar chart in exercise 2.

_____

_____

_____

_____

_____

_____

How to say it or write it
The cartoon deals with …   I think the artist's depiction of the … is intended to / is aimed at making / conveys …   The artist wants to say / express the idea that …   The point of the cartoon seems to be that …

_____

_____

_____

_____

_____

_____

_____

_____

_____

Writing workshop 1

Do after Section F

1 Read the text below and say what the following percentages refer to.

26% → _____   40% → _____

31% → _____

If Gen Z want their American Dream to have a happy ending – it is time to start planning now for retirement.

If you are anything like me, an American 20-something Gen Zer, then the chances are you think too much about living for the moment and think everything the 'oldies' do is wrong. OK, they have left the planet in a mess and their
5 fashion-sense is so … ugh! But look at those seniors who are enjoying their retirement: always on vacation, posting selfies in exotic locations, moving to places like Florida to relax and enjoy the sun. They are living the lifestyle that everyone seems to think we young people live!

10 How many of you think you will be able to live like that in your seventies and beyond? Have you even thought about it? Some of you have. According to recent surveys, around a quarter of Gen Zers do not believe they will be able to rely on social security in retirement and just under a third think they will have to work in some form after retirement age. To those of you
15 who have not thought that far ahead, it is crucial that you start – *NOW!*
Sociologists are describing us as the 'sandwich generation'. Not because we love *Subway* but because our generation will face a double challenge. Not only will we have to look after our own children, who we are having later in life, we will also have to wait longer to inherit any wealth our parents may leave us because they are living well into their eighties and nineties! And that is if
20 they have not sold their house and spent their remaining money on their own healthcare!
A lot of us, me – a freelance journalist – included, do not stay with one employer, or even in one career, for our working lives and many of us work in the gig economy with little or no pension benefits, so if we expect to have any sort of retirement, we urgently need to start planning now. You know what they say: fail to plan, plan to … be poor, or something like that. You know who you
25 are! For every ten US Gen Zers reading this, four of you have no retirement savings at all yet.
So, do what I've done: talk to a financial adviser, begin putting a few dollars away and get into the habit of saving. It is not too late. And in thirty or forty years from now, who knows, maybe we will meet each other on the beach in Florida!

(413 words)

2 Write in the right label for each of the examples from the text.

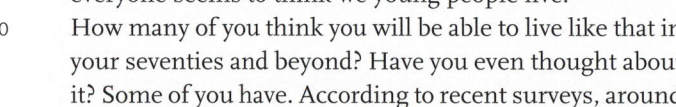

call to action | direct address of the reader | informal, humorous tone | rhetorical question | strong, emotive language

line 1: *If you are anything like me, …*   _____

lines 4–5: *… their fashion sense is so … ugh!*   _____

lines 11–12: *Have you even thought about it?*   _____

line 15 & 23: *crucial; urgently*   _____

line 26: *So, do what I've done: …*   _____

3 Look at the illustration on the previous page. <u>Underline</u> the correct alternative in the following sentences to make them true

  1 The cartoon accompanying the text **reflects / doesn't reflect** the overall tone of the article, i.e. a serious message conveyed with a touch of humour.

  2 While the author makes an effort to show that he/she is the same generation as his/her Gen Z readers, the cartoon **underlines / undermines** this because the main character, wearing a business suit, is clearly not a Gen Zer.

  3 The accountant's statement in the speech bubble employs **exaggeration / understatement** to emphasize the difficulty the worker faces in saving enough for retirement.

  4 It would also seem to **support / contradict** the author of the article's main point because the red-haired man clearly has not saved enough money for retirement.

  5 The choice of cartoon, however, **has the advantage / runs the risk** of conveying an overly pessimistic view of the future and may discourage rather than encourage readers to follow the author's advice.

4 Analyse how the author tries to persuade the reader of his/her point of view. Refer to structure, language and the illustration printed with the article.

Look at your student's book pages 213–218 and the PagePlayer App for more help.

> **How to say it or write it.**
>
> **Referring to structure**
> Introduction → The author begins by engaging readers with … / challenging readers to … / raising the point that …
>
> Main body → The main body of the article comprises two / three / … paragraphs containing his/her arguments, namely, …
>
> The author supports his/her view that … by making two / three / … points which are each dealt with in a paragraph
>
> Conclusion → The author concludes his/her article with a call to action / a plea to his/her readers / by posing a question …

> **How to say it or write it.**
>
> **Referring to cartoons**
> Describing it → The cartoon shows … / The scene depicts … The caption / speech bubble says … In the foreground / background / centre, there is / are …
>
> Interpreting it → The cartoon deals with … The point of the cartoon is / seems to be … The humour lies in the exaggeration of / extreme situation …
>
> Comparing a cartoon and a text → Although the cartoon shows …, the text says … The cartoon supports the author's message in the following way(s) … The cartoon offers a similar / different opinion to the text.

Writing workshop 2

Do after Section F

1 The statements below are about the text 'Nothing more than a dream' (SB, pages 155–157). Complete each of the statements using the correct connective.

> although • but • despite • however • nevertheless

1 The article examines the 'American Dream' – the new versus the old. _____,

it seems to me that there is not very much that is uniquely American about the issues raised in

the text.

2 _____ listing all the disadvantages faced by young American workers today,

the author does not suggest any solutions and seems only to say we should not judge young

people if they accept this 'new American Dream'.

3 _____ the author says vocational schools have increased in popularity,

he/she writes that the new American Dream celebrates 'play', not vocations – this does not

make sense.

4 The text claims that the gig worker is America's 'cultural response' to the reduction in job

security, _____ I think the gig economy is a creation of businesses seeking

greater profits, not of culture.

5 The text talks about a 'new American Dream'. After reading the text, _____,

I do not think it is clear what this new dream actually is.

2 Read the text 'Nothing more than a dream' (SB, pages 155–157) again. Examine which themes conveyed in the article correspond to the information displayed in the bar chart below. Make notes on the key words below and on the next page.

American adults were asked: "What does the American Dream mean to you?"

Personal freedom	66%
Religious freedom	56%
Equality	55%
Security	54%
The pursuit of happiness	53%
Economic freedom	51%

Source: Statista, 2017

Personal freedom:

_____

Religious freedom:

_____

Equality:

_____

Security:

_____

The pursuit of happiness:

_____

Economic freedom:

_____

3 The phrases below are very useful for writing formal texts such as a letter to an editor, but before you can use them, you must first <u>underline</u> the correct form of the verbs.

1 I **write / am writing** in response to the article which appeared in your newspaper on …

2 It makes sense **to start / starting** by **to ask / asking** whether …

3 There are several questions to think about when **to discuss / discussing** the issue of …

4 Another point **to consider / considering** is this: …

5 The author seems **to say / saying** that … despite **to provide / providing** no concrete evidence …

6 I **believe / am believing** strongly that …

7 I would like to suggest **to reconsider / reconsidering** how we treat the subject of …

4 Using more formal vocabulary can improve your writing. Rewrite the following sentences about the text on pages 155–157 using the correct alternative from the box for the highlighted words. Change the form of any verbs if needed.

bemoan | continue to be | overly | pose | previous | provide | purpose | repeatedly |
require | state | subsequently

1 In my view, the author **asks** a lot of questions in the article but does not **give** any constructive answers.

2 The author **says** that the American Dream was "truly gettable" for **earlier** generations but **afterwards** contradicts this claim by saying this was not true for a "large number" of Americans.

3 The author **again and again** writes that the current generation of young people just want to have freedom and fun, but I believe this is **too** simplistic.

4 The text spends a lot of time saying life was difficult for most people in the past and life **is still** difficult for most people today – I do not see any **point** in **crying about** that. We **need** more optimism, not less.

5 Write a letter to the editor commenting on the author's views of the 'New American Dream'. You may write from your own perspective or from the perspective of a young American. Use phrases from exercise 1 and the information from the bar chart in exercise 2 and/or from your work in class to support your views.

Look at your student's book pages 167–172 and the PagePlayer App for more help.

Dealing with listening tasks

Do after Section B

Gun control in the US

Task type: sentence completion

🔊 05

1 In this type of task, you must listen for specific details. You may be asked to listen for statistics in the form of numbers and percentages. It is helpful to know the different ways to express these. Listen and circle the number or amount closest to what the speaker says.

> Look at your student's book pages 123–125 and the PagePlayer App for more help.

Example: 1 *"just under two-thirds"*

1 67%	68%	(65%)
2 15	20%	¼
3 three and a half	3,500,000	3.5
4 53%	49%	100%
5 81%	18%	four-fifths
6 26%	33%	50%
7 a significant majority	half	a significant minority

2 a The sentences you must complete usually contain synonyms for key words used in the listening text. For sentences 1–3 below, (circle) the words that best match the meaning of the key words in red. You will complete the gaps in exercise 3.

1 In his opening **comments**, the US president said gun violence was **an American** shame, calling

it _____ .   remarks   talks   patriot   national

2 Although everyone condemns shooting deaths, America's people and their **public**

representatives, in particular, remain **divided** over the issue of _____ .

statesmen   politicians   polarized   separated

3 44% of Republican voters own **firearms**, while the number for Democrat **voters** is

only _____ .

weapons   guns   supporters   opponents   just   alone

b For sentences 4–6, think of and write in synonyms for the key words in blue.

4 Around two-thirds of gun owners have guns for **self-defense**, **40%** for hunting or sport, while

one in twenty said they needed a gun _____ .

self-defense: _____ 40%: _____ one in twenty: _____

5 **Over half** of Americans **state** that gun laws **should** be _____ .

over half: _____ state: _____ should: _____

6 Half of Republicans think **present** gun laws shouldn't be **altered** and 25% even

support _____ .

present: _____ altered: _____ support: _____

🔊 06

3 Now listen to the audio and complete sentences 1–6 in exercises 2 a and b.

48

Words in context

1   Read the text about political divisions in the United States.

The *dis*United States: The American Dream *Nightmare*

A recent Hollywood movie depicts a group of Washington politicians conspiring to spark a war between the United States and Russia. Why? Because they think the US needs an external adversary to unify its people. As one character
5   says, Americans' 'problem today is half the country thinks the other half is its enemy because we have no one else to fight'. The plot is the stuff of fantasy, of course, but that quote doesn't seem so far from reality.

At President Biden's inauguration in 2021, there were no cheering crowds for two reasons: one,
10   the Covid-19 pandemic, and two, being just two weeks after the January 6th insurrection at Capitol Hill, there were fears of a repeat attempt to disrupt the peaceful transfer of power. Washington was locked down and patrolled by the American military, troops slept overnight in the Capitol building. Before January 6th, 2021, we thought we would see only see such scenes in a Hollywood movie, but now it was reality.

15   Today's America is split down the middle and each side has its 'alternative facts' – a phrase first used by a spokesperson for President Trump. Some people laughed when she first said it, but nobody is laughing now. Look at the November 2020 election: Democrats point to numerous court judgements and the FBI's statement that there was no electoral fraud, yet a majority of Republicans believe Biden is an illegitimate president and Trump supporters call Biden's victory
20   the 'Big Lie'. Republicans ask why Democrats condemn the violence of January 6th, 2021, but not the violence which occurred during the Black Lives Matter protests. During one of these protests, Kyle Rittenhouse, then aged 17, shot two people dead and injured a third. Acquitted of murder and set free by a court, those on the right-wing claim him as a patriotic hero, but he is denounced as a homicidal vigilante by those on the left-wing. There is no objective 'truth', each side has its
25   own version of reality.

In his campaign and his inaugural address, Biden promised to revive bipartisan politics during his presidency, but his efforts by the time of writing (May 2022) have produced only one major piece of legislation: the Bipartisan Infrastructure Bill. Bipartisan? Barely. 62% of Republican senators and 94% of Republican House representatives voted *against* it. How realistic is it to ex-
30   pect bipartisanship from Republicans? Democrats twice impeached their president, some even claimed he was a Russian spy. The hostility between the sides in America has even poisoned public discourse: Robert de Niro said 'F**k Trump' on live TV in 2018; during a live TV broadcast, a father replied to President Biden's *Christmas* greeting with the words 'Let's go, Brandon' – a code phrase on the right meaning 'F**k you, Biden'. In the US, using curse words on live TV used
35   to be absolutely taboo, yet now they are used to insult Presidents! America, it seems, is no longer a melting pot, but a *boiling* pot, and a pot that is boiling over.

A new genre of books on America's bookshelves would seem to bear this out: books about American disintegration. Barbara F Walter, an author and professor of political science, in her book *How Civil Wars Start*, argues that the US is currently a mix between democracy and
40   autocracy, with the country heading the wrong way towards autocracy. Another book, *Divided We Fall* warns of states seceding from the union, an option favoured by 52% of Trump and 41% of Biden voters in a recent survey. As we approach the 250th birthday of the United States in 2026, the question posed by Abraham Lincoln in his 1863 Gettysburg address: 'whether that nation … can long endure' seems very relevant today.

(611 words)

---

to **depict** *darstellen*

to **spark** *auslösen, anzünden*

insurrection *Aufstand, Aufruhr*

transfer of power *Machtübergabe*

spokesperson *Pressesprecher/in*

numerous *zahlreich*

electoral fraud *Wahlfälschung*

illegitimate *rechtswidrig*

to **condemn sb/sth** *jdn/etw verurteilen/ missbilligen*

to **acquit sb** *jdn für unschuldig erklären*

to **denounce sb/sth** *jdn/etw anprangern*

homicidal *mörderisch*

vigilante *Mitglied einer Bürgerwehr*

to **revive** *wiederbeleben, auffrischen*

bipartisan *Zweiparteien-*

bill *Gesetzesvorlage*

barely *kaum*

hostility *Feindseligkeit*

public discourse *gesellschaftlicher Diskurs*

to **insult** *beleidigen*

to **boil (over)** *(über-)kochen, sieden*

to **bear sth out** *etw bestätigen*

to **argue** *behaupten*

to **head towards sth** *sich (zu-) bewegen auf etw*

to **endure** *(an-)dauern*

2   You can find the highlighted words from the text on page 49 in the table below.
Fill in the empty boxes in the following wordlist.

Word/Phrase	Memory support	German
legislation	**WORD FAMILY** to _____ (v) _____ (adj) _____ (n)	Gesetzgebung
_____	**COLLOCATIONS** ~ party, coalition, movement, ideas, intellectual, extremists, extremism, terrorists	rechts-/linksorientiert, linker/rechter Flügel
to _____	**WORD FAMILY** conspiracy (n) conspirator (n)	sich verschwören
to _____	**SENTENCE:** Although the people of Quebec chose not to _____ from Canada in 1995, there is still a lot of support for independence.	sich absondern
to condemn	**SENTENCE:** _____ _____	jdn/etw verurteilen/missbilligen
adversary	**SYNONYM(S):** _____ _____	Gegner/in, Feind

3   Which words from 'Words in context' fit in the sentences below? The lines show the number of letters.

1 There are **n** __ __ __ __ __ __ __ issues which divide American society: politics, guns, abortion, to name a few.

2 Each mass shooting **r** __ __ __ __ __ __ the movement for gun law reform, but reform never happens.

3 Some Americans **d** __ __ __ __ __ __ __ kneeling during the national anthem as unpatriotic and disrespectful.

4 When you think about it, superhero movies are all about **v** __ __ __ __ __ __ __ __ **s** in colourful costumes.

5 650,000 undocumented immigrants are waiting for the DREAM act to be passed by Congress and become a **b** __ __ __ .

4   Pronounce these words from 'Words in context', writing down the correct spelling.

[ɪlɪˈdʒɪtɪmɪt] _____   [ˌɪnsəˈrɛkʃən] _____

[ˈpʌblɪk ˈdɪskɔːs] _____   [hɒsˈtɪlɪti] _____

[baɪˌpɑːtɪˈzæn] _____   [ˈprɛzɪdənsi] _____

The chill out zone

1 Not very presidential

Three of the five quotes below were said by US presidents and two weren't. Tick the boxes.

Real   Fake

1 *(About broccoli)* I haven't liked it since I was a little kid. And my mother made me eat it. And I'm president of the United States. And I'm not gonna eat any more broccoli!

2 *(About himself)* Actually, throughout my life, my two greatest assets have been mental stability and being, like, really smart – [a] genius … and a very stable genius at that!

3 *(About the French President)* He's a nice guy, but his English is really crap.

4 *(About a journalist)* What a stupid son of a bitch!

5 *(About the UK)* The UK is cool. I love the Brits. They have a queen. We should have a king. Me!!

Bonus! Write the number of the quote and the name of each of the three presidents.
TIP: Put the quote into an internet search.

_____   _____   _____

2 Musical grammar

In each of these songs by North American artists you will find examples of the grammar points studied in Topic 4. Find the songs online. Listen to them and, if possible, read the lyrics. Which grammar points do you hear the singers use in the parts shown?

1 Eminem – Lose Yourself   *The first three lines*   _____

2 Taylor Swift – I Knew You Were Trouble   *The first verse*   _____

3 The Weeknd – Alone Again   *Verses 2-4*   _____

4 Lil Nas X – Void   *second verse*   _____

3 Crossword puzzle

a Each of the six words in the puzzle are taken from Sections A–F of Topic 4. The page number where the word appears in your student's book is given in brackets after the clue.

1 First name of the US president in office from 2001–2009. (p. 153)

2 This can be used by people to sell a gun in the US without holding a firearm license: gun show … (p. 143)

3 A former slave who campaigned to abolish slavery: Frederick … (p. 146)

4 The … Dream (p. 155)

5 A program that allows undocumented people who arrived in the US as children to work (p. 149)

6 The Constitution and the Bill of … form the basis of the government of the United States. (p. 136)

b The letters in the green boxes will give you the family name of a person from Section G.

51

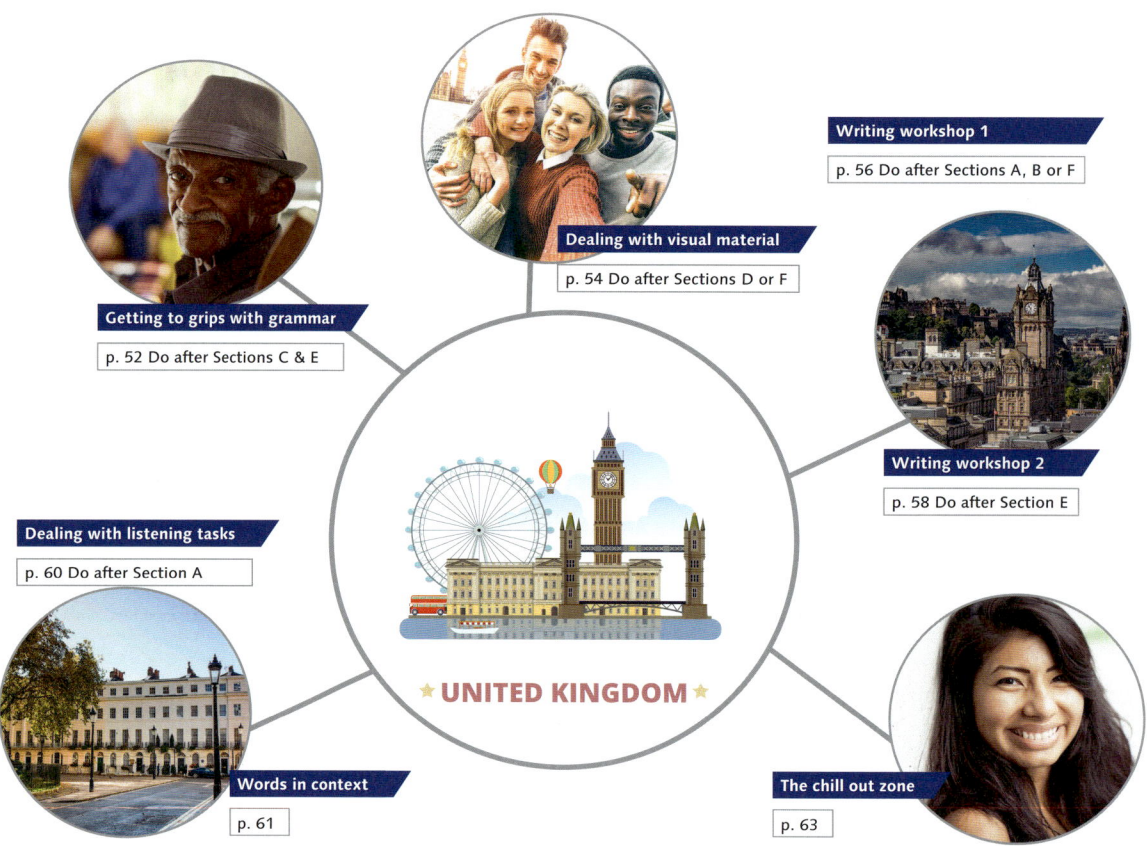

Getting to grips with grammar

Do after Section C

G ▶ *The past perfect, SB, p. 285*

1 The simple past and past perfect

The sentences below and on page 53 are about Anthony Brown, who you read about on pages 191–192 of your student's book. Complete them by putting one of the verbs into the simple past and one into the past perfect.

1 Anthony Brown's father *had already returned* (already return) to the UK when Anthony *was* (be)

   born in 1960.

2 Anthony _____ (come) to the UK with his mother and siblings after his

   father _____ (work) and saved money for six years to pay for the journey.

3 Due to new legislation in 1971, Anthony _____ (lose) his UK citizenship because he

   _____ (spend) four years studying back in Jamaica.

4 Inspired by anger at police behaviour he _____ (see) on TV, Anthony

   _____ (decide) he should study law and join the police.

5 He _____ (apply) to university before he _____ (learn) about his

   immigration status.

6 He _____ (receive) a letter telling him that the UK authorities _____

   (classify) him as an immigration offender.

7 A campaign to stop Brown's deportation _____ **(be)** successful, but the whole

experience _____ **(shake)** him.

8 However, he _____ **(learn)** from it too, and Brown _____ **(decide)** to use

his experience to help others threatened with deportation.

Do after Section E

2 Adjectives and adverbs

G ▸ *Adjectives and adverbs, SB, p. 293*

Complete the description of the graph showing Scottish support for and opposition to independence by using the adjective <u>or</u> adverb form of the adjectives in the box.

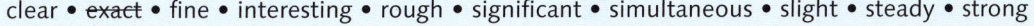

clear • ~~exact~~ • fine • interesting • rough • significant • simultaneous • slight • steady • strong

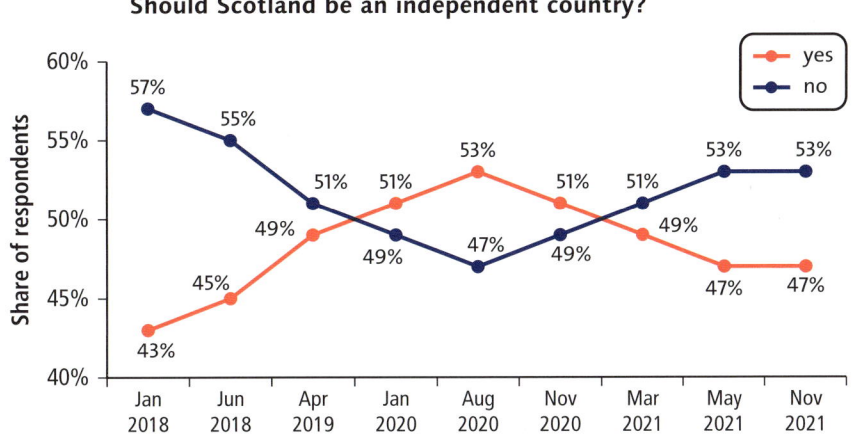

Should Scotland be an independent country?

Details: United Kingdom (Scotland); November 18–22, 2021; 1,060 respondents; 16 years and older; Scottish adults © Statista 2022

The two lines on the graph mirror each other almost **1.** _____*exactly*_____. At the beginning of

the graph in January 2018, Scottish people expressed **2.** _____ opposition to

independence, with 57% against. In the following two years, however, support for Scottish

independence rose **3.** _____, gaining 10%. **4.** _____, at two points

in the graph, support for and opposition to independence were **5.** _____ balanced at

50% for and against. After August 2020, support fell and opposition rose **6.** _____

so that for most of 2020 there was a **7.** _____ majority of people expressing support

for independence for the only time in the period covered by the graph. Opposition to independence

reached its lowest level in August 2020 and then **8.** _____ recovered over the next

nine months. The end of the graph in November 2021 shows the position **9.** _____

the same as at the beginning although there was a **10.** _____ decrease of 4% in the

majority against independence.

Dealing with visual material

Do after Sections D or F

British identity

In exercises 1–3, you will practise describing graphs focusing on British identity and drawing conclusions from the information they present. In exercises 4–5 you will comment on visual and textual information related to Brexit.

Look at your student's book pages 43–44 and the PagePlayer App for more help.

1 In your exercise book, answer the following questions on figure A.

    1 What type of visual representation is it?

    2 What does it depict?

    3 What is its source?

2 Now write sentences describing what happens to the statistics in figure A for the following groups at the following times:

    1 EU immigration from 2012 until 2015

    2 EU immigration in the first half of 2016

    3 EU immigration after the Brexit referendum in June 2016

    4 Non-EU immigration in relation to EU immigration in 2016 H2

    5 Non-EU immigration since 2016

    6 Total immigration from 2017 to 2019

Figure A
Number of immigrants entering the United Kingdom from 2012 to 2019, by citizenship (in 1,000s)

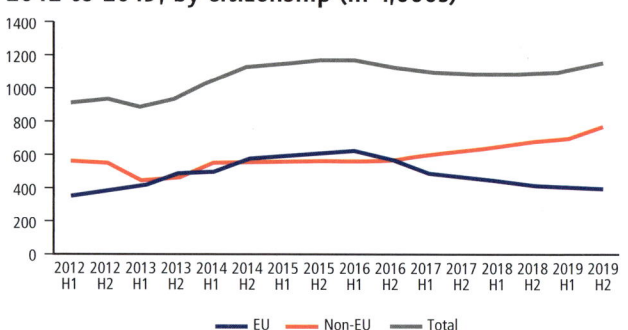

Details: United Kingdom; House of Commons; Office for National Statistics (UK) © Statista 2022

3 In your exercise book, answer the following questions on figure B.

    1 What kind of visual representation is it?

    2 What is it divided into?

4 Assuming the trends in figure A continue into the future, what conclusions can you draw from figures A and B in terms of:

    1 the effect of Brexit in reducing immigration?

    2 the likely make-up of the immigrant community in the UK?

Figure B
Birth region/country of non-British UK residents in 2021 (compiled from top 20 countries of birth)

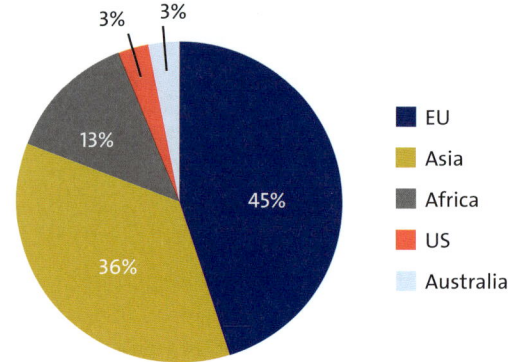

Source: Office of National Statistics, UK Government; www.ons.gov.uk

Britain's relationship to the EU: Brexit

5 Look at figures C and D and the quotation below. Then do the task which follows.

Figure C
Number of police recorded religious hate crimes in England and Wales from 2011/12 to 2020/21

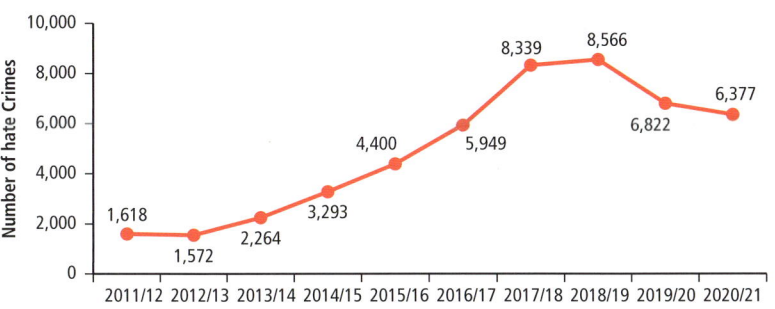

Details: United Kingdom (England, Wales); UK
Home Office; April 1, 2011 to March 31, 2021

Figure D
Victims of religious hate crimes in England and Wales 2021

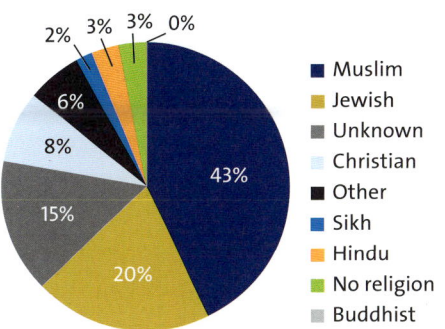

> I think Brexit has certainly made us a meaner and nastier country. Brexit poisoned the atmosphere.

– Lord Dubs, British politician and former child refugee

Task: You will have to comment on the quotation. Before you start, make rough notes on the arguments which support or do not support the opinion expressed in the quotation.

Support the quotation	Do not support the quotation
– it can't be a coincidence that the hate crime figures began to rise in 2012/13 – the same year the whole Brexit debate began	– the graph on religious hate crimes shows a downward trend – maybe the situation is improving

6 Now use your notes to write your comment on the quote in exercise 5.

How to say it or write it

Describing pie charts:	Describing line graphs:
The pie chart is divided into … segments / sections …	to reach a peak / a low point of …
Each segment represents …	to remain constant / stable
The sections representing … and … constitute the majority …	to increase / rise / grow / go up … by … to …
… makes up the biggest / smallest segment.	to decrease / fall / drop / go down … by … to …
more than / roughly / about twice as much as …	an increase / a rise / growth …
far less than …	sharp(ly) / steep(ly) / sudden(ly) / constant(ly) / gradual(ly) / slight(ly) / slow(ly)

Writing workshop 1

Do after Sections A, B or F

British identity and attitudes to Britain's colonial past

Look at your student's book page 42 and the PagePlayer App for more help.

1 Read the text on page 57. Use a monolingual dictionary to find the meaning of the following words as used in the text. Write definitions in your exercise book.

acquit (l. 1)	vociferous (l. 15)	reckoning with (l. 32)	set its face (l. 37)
flesh (l. 12)	Victorian (l. 29)	sought to (l. 34)	acknowledging (l. 42)
prosecution (l. 14)	offence (l. 31)		

2 It is important to examine the words in a task carefully. Read the example task below and then tick (✓) four statements (1–6) which you think should be included in an answer to the task.

> Outline the historical background to the issues discussed in the text and summarize the reasons the author gives for his / her position.

Look at your student's book page 81 and the PagePlayer App for more help.

1 Many British public places have monuments to the British Empire which celebrate people like the slave-trader Edward Colston – these reflect 19th century values and beliefs. ☐

2 The Black Lives Matter movement was inspired by police killings of Black people in the US. ☐

3 Many local people campaigned for a long time to make changes to historic monuments that would put them in context, for example to change the plaque on the Colston statue which described him as "virtuous and wise". ☐

4 I think the author makes good arguments in support of acknowledging historic injustice. ☐

5 The author says the UK government is wrong to focus only on celebrating the positive sides of British heritage and should not oppose all attempts to educate people about the negative sides. ☐

6 The author argues that the fact that the Colston statue is now in a Bristol museum shows that removing statues from public places is not the same as deleting British history. ☐

3 Being a summary, your text must use as few words as possible while also being informative. In your exercise book, rewrite these long sentences about the text in as short a way as possible. Before you start, look at the example and examine the ways in which the meaning has been expressed using fewer words and how some words have been left out.

1 The author makes the point that it is not a good idea for the government to punish crimes which are committed during public protests with longer prison sentences and that they should think about other ways of punishing offenders such as voluntary work. (43 words)

The author says the government should avoid longer sentences for crimes committed during public protests and instead consider restorative justice. (20 words)

2 The text gives a description of how in the 19th century some authorities in some places in Britain such as Bristol thought people like Edward Colston, a slave trader from Britain in the 17th century, should be honoured for their actions.

3 One of the arguments made by the text is that the decision of the jury shows that members of the public in Britain are aware that a lot of public monuments can send messages that are old-fashioned and that have values from the 19th century.

4 The author does not hold the opinion that the case of the "Colston Four" gives everybody permission to cause damage to every public monument or statue because the issue in Bristol was one of a kind and had been going on for a long time.

4 Now do the task. You may write a completely new summary or include parts of the previous exercises in your answer.

> Outline the historical background to the issues discussed in the text and summarize the reasons the author gives for his / her position.

EDITORIAL The Guardian view on the 'Colston Four': taking racism down

Good to know

restorative justice: ein System der Strafjustiz, das sich auf die Rehabilitation von Straftätern durch Versöhnung mit den Opfern und der Gemeinschaft konzentriert.

woke: Der Begriff „woke" wird von seinen Anhängern verwendet, um auf Ungerechtigkeit und Diskriminierung aufmerksam zu sein, wird aber von einigen abwertend verwendet, da sie ihn für einen liberalen Trend halten, der nicht echt ist.

The decision by a jury in Bristol to acquit the "Colston Four" of criminal damage, following their role in the toppling of a statue of the slave trader Edward Colston in June 2020, is a welcome sign that Britain is changing. In the 17th century Colston was one
5 of Britain's wealthiest slave traders. It speaks volumes about what Bristol's Victorian civic leaders valued when they decided to erect a monument to Colston in 1895, almost a century after the slave trade was abolished (decades before slavery itself). Just 12 years earlier, a second statue of William Wilberforce, who campaigned
10 for slavery's abolition, was erected in his home city of Hull. Yet in the south-western English port, whose wealth was built on the flesh trade, it was seen as fit to honour Colston with a monument, and a plaque describing him as "virtuous and wise".

The prosecution should never have been brought, and perhaps
15 would not have been had the home secretary, Priti Patel, and other ministers, been less vociferous in their condemnations of the protests, which culminated in Colston's statue being dumped in the harbour. It is far from clear that this use of the state's resources was in the public interest. Six other activists were dealt with via a "restorative justice" route, including voluntary work.

Objections to the Colston statue, which occupied a prominent position in Bristol's centre, were
20 longstanding, and part of a wider, local movement to remove tributes to the slave trader from the city (including the renaming of its main concert hall). That feelings among a section of the public finally boiled over was because of the passionate objections to racial injustice aroused by the Black Lives Matter demonstrations following the murder, less than two weeks earlier, of George Floyd.

The verdict is not, as one of the defendants herself pointed out, a green light to "start pulling
25 down all the statues in the UK". Colston was a particular person. His monument belongs to a specific time and place – and is now in a Bristol museum, thus demolishing the idea that taking it down was an effort to "erase" the past. What the jury's decision shows is that members of the public are more than willing to think about the messages embedded in our built environment, including monuments – so many of them Victorian. They accepted the defence's case that it was
30 the presence of the statue, and failure to update the plaque, that constituted a moral – if not a legal – offence.

Reckoning with the past is difficult. Britain was once an empire that governed vast areas of the world. Astonishing levels of greed and cruelty are part of our history, along with a religiously motivated "civilising" mission that sought to export Christianity across the globe. Everyone who
35 cares about knowledge should support efforts to increase public understanding of all this. In organisations across the country, including the National Trust, good work is being done.

Yet up to now, the government has set its face against anything that might make heritage less celebratory, condemning as "woke" all attempts to place artefacts such as those that fill British country houses (and city squares) in a broader context. Its repressive police bill seeks to increase
40 prison sentences dramatically for those convicted of criminal damage (at present, the maximum for causing damage worth less than £5,000 is three months).

Statues are symbols, and tackling racism requires more than moving them. But acknowledging historic injustices is part of building a more equal society today. Rather than complaining about the way in which the law has been applied, as some ministers have done, the government as a
45 whole should think again. Britain is better off without Bristol's monument to Colston.

(433 words)   Source: *The Guardian*, 7 January 2022

Writing workshop 2

Do after Section E

Look at your student's book pages 167–172 and the PagePlayer App for more help.

1 Below you will find a comment task with a sample answer. Some parts are missing. The introduction is missing a connector and each paragraph needs a topic sentence. Choose a sentence from each of the five pairs on page 59 and write them in the gaps A–E.

Should Scotland be an independent country? Comment on the issue of Scottish independence, referring to the cartoon and quotation and any relevant background knowledge you have.

"It seems the Scottish people can't make up their minds. The most recent opinion poll in May 2022 saw 47% against and 45% for independence. However, for leading Scottish businesspeople, the case for independence definitely has not been made. Uncertainty surrounds a number of vital issues including currency, regulation, tax, pensions, EU membership and support for our exports around the world; and uncertainty is bad for business."

Sample answer:

The issue of Scottish independence has not gone away despite the clear 'No' vote given in answer to the question "Should Scotland be an independent country?" in the 2014 referendum. The statistics and the quotation seem to imply that, financially at least, no was the right answer, but the cartoon implies that the question is still open. One has to wonder though if such a question can be decided only in terms of cold, hard cash or will the Scottish heart choose a different answer.

A _____

B _____

Although the 'No' side might lead at the moment, the 'Yes' side has never dropped below 40% since the referendum. That is a lot of unhappiness in the UK relationship. Divorces, however, can be expensive. The UK is Scotland's largest trading partner. If Scotland were to leave the UK, and even rejoin the EU, it would be joining what is currently a smaller market and putting trading barriers between it and the UK.

C _____

_____

Independence would mean economic problems, they say; a new border would affect travel; a small country cannot survive outside its big neighbour, and so on. Brexit has economic consequences for Britain, but a majority still voted for it. National identity means more to people than economic forecasts. Scotland has the most educated population in Europe. That means they have a good chance of overcoming the challenges of independence.

D _____

During the Corona pandemic, Boris Johnson pointed to the vaccine deals that the UK was able to secure, and Scotland benefitted from these too. At a time when Finland and Sweden are joining NATO and some Eastern European countries are applying to join the EU, now would not seem to be the best time for Scotland to disrupt its society, health or defence systems by voting to leave the UK.

E

There is no countdown clock running on the independence question. After all, the last referendum was not that long ago and, based on the opinion polls, a referendum tomorrow would not produce a clear majority, yes or no. The world and the global economy are still recovering from the effects of a pandemic and that has not been helped by the tragedy in Ukraine and tensions between East and West. The Scottish people alone will decide, but maybe they should wait before posing the question again.

- The cartoon clearly depicts a couple who are communicating constructively.
- The cartoon evokes an image of an unhappy marriage and those often end in divorce.

- Speed, in my opinion, is most important.
- Timing, in my opinion, is the key issue.

- It is ironic that the arguments made by the anti-independence side sound a lot like the 'Remain' side in the Brexit referendum.
- It is ironic that Scotland voted against independence and against Brexit.

- I am going to have a look at this tough subject.
- Let us examine this emotive issue.

- Nevertheless, one has to ask what good has being part of the UK done for Scotland recently.
- Nevertheless, during times of wider global risks, the benefits of being a member of a multinational group would seem to be stronger.

2 Now write a comment on 'Dexit' – a German exit from the EU. Refer to the material below and any research that you want to carry out.

"Brexit has shown that leaving the EU is possible. Germany should not be afraid to ask itself if continuing this European experiment is really in its best interest."

Germany: Are you satisfied with the way democracy works in the EU?

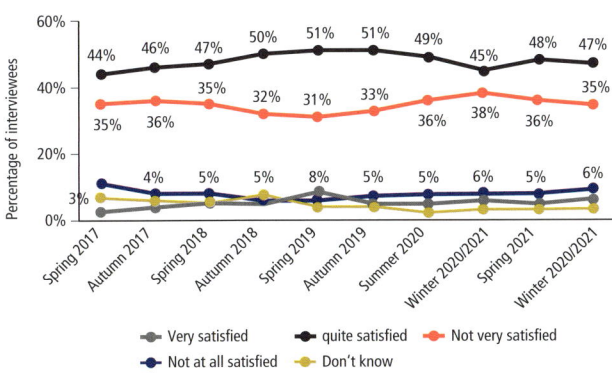

Which Countries are EU Contributors and Beneficiaries?
Net contributions to the EU budget,
by member state (2018, in million euros)*

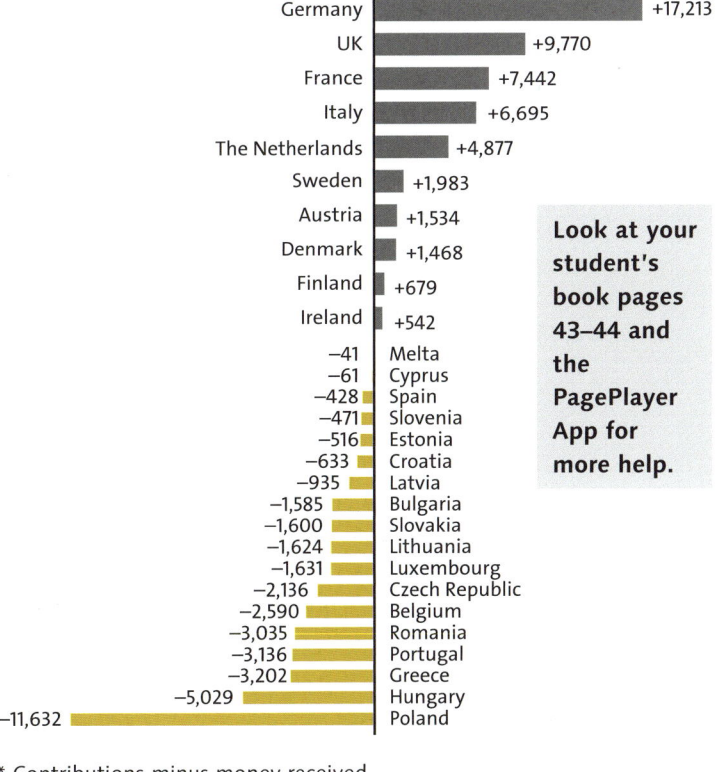

Germany	+17,213
UK	+9,770
France	+7,442
Italy	+6,695
The Netherlands	+4,877
Sweden	+1,983
Austria	+1,534
Denmark	+1,468
Finland	+679
Ireland	+542
−41	Melta
−61	Cyprus
−428	Spain
−471	Slovenia
−516	Estonia
−633	Croatia
−935	Latvia
−1,585	Bulgaria
−1,600	Slovakia
−1,624	Lithuania
−1,631	Luxembourg
−2,136	Czech Republic
−2,590	Belgium
−3,035	Romania
−3,136	Portugal
−3,202	Greece
−5,029	Hungary
−11,632	Poland

* Contributions minus money received
Source: European Commission

Look at your student's book pages 43–44 and the PagePlayer App for more help.

GERMANY'S MOST IMPORTANT TRADING PARTNERS IN 2021

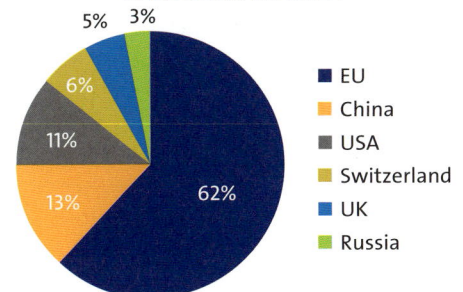

- EU 62%
- China 13%
- USA 11%
- Switzerland 6%
- UK 5%
- Russia 3%

Statista, 2022

Look at your student's book pages 123–125 and the PagePlayer App for more help.

Dealing with listening tasks

Do after Section A

The British Empire

Task type: multiple matching

In this type of task, you are given some short headings and have to match them to the correct speaker, but you must be careful because there will be some extra headings that you do not need.

1 Read the listening task in exercise 3 below carefully. Using a monolingual dictionary, look up the meanings of these words/phrases from the task. Write in the meaning you think applies to the content of the listening task.

Look at your student's book page 42 and the PagePlayer App for more help.

1 to throw the baby out with the bathwater _____

2 tangible _____

3 to make amends _____

4 to own up to sth _____

5 monopoly _____

6 pinnacle _____

7 to have enough on your plate _____

2 The British Empire is the topic of the listening task. Circle the vocabulary in the box that is relevant to the topic. Thinking about the topic will help 'activate' your background knowledge.

> exploitation • genocide • Jim Crow era • proportional representation • reparations •
> plantations • the Suffragettes • Shakespeare • colonies • prohibition • slavery • free trade

🔊 07

3 Now it is time to do the listening task.

You will hear five British people give their views on the legacy of the British Empire. While listening, match the headings A to G with the speakers 1 to 5. There are two more headings than you need. You now have time to read the assignment.

	Heading
A	We shouldn't throw the baby out with the bathwater.
B	We should concentrate on tangible efforts to make amends now.
C	Pride in the Empire is for right-wing nationalists.
D	Owning up to our shame shows respect to the victims.
E	No colonial power had a monopoly on terrible behaviour.
F	The British Empire was the pinnacle of civilization.
G	What's done is done; we have enough on our plate today.

Speaker	1	2	3	4	5
Heading					

Now listen to the recording again.

Words in context

1 Read about a royal visit to the Caribbean and then do the exercises which follow.

'Perfect storm': royals misjudged Caribbean tour, say critics

It was supposed to be a visit to mark the Queen's platinum jubilee – a chance to present the modern face of the British monarchy to a region where republican sentiment is on the rise. But it really didn't turn out that way. [...] Calls for slavery reparations and the enduring fury of the Windrush scandal followed [the Duke and Duchess of Cambridge] across Belize, Jamaica and the
5 Bahamas – overshadowing a trip aimed at strengthening the Commonwealth and discouraging other countries from following Barbados's example in becoming a republic.

Upon arrival in Belize, the couple were met with protests from villagers over a land dispute involving a charity William is a patron of. In Jamaica, the prime minister told them in an awkward meeting that the country would be "moving on" to become a republic, and a government
10 committee in the Bahamas urged the royals to issue "a full and formal apology for their crimes against humanity". [...]

"This was another photo opportunity, and rather presumptuous to assume that Jamaican people were suddenly going to welcome William and his wife with open arms," said Velma McClymont, a writer and former Caribbean studies academic who was born in Jamaica and was five when the
15 country gained independence. [...] Followers of the trip in the UK may have gained a different impression. On Friday, the Sun reserved its front page for the tour, gushing that "Kate dazzles on Jamaica tour" and suggesting that the pair had "touched hearts". [...] The same could not be said of the coverage in the Jamaican media. "It was dubbed in [the UK] media as a charm offensive, but I'm not quite so sure it came off that way. It wasn't a royal failure, but I wouldn't quite deem
20 it a regal success either," said Tyrone Reid, an associate editor at national newspaper the Jamaica Gleaner. Reid added that local publications had devoted considerable column inches to the views of "a growing number of Jamaicans demanding the British monarch and British state apologise for and accept its role in the abhorrent slave trade of years ago."

[...] Philip Murphy, a professor at the University of London and former director of the Institute of
25 Commonwealth Studies, [...] pointed to the growing emphasis on the relationship between colonialism and racial oppression after the Black Lives Matter movement, along with damage to the royals' reputations after Meghan Markle's accusations of racism and the British government through the Windrush scandal. "All of those things make it politically very difficult to stage this visit at this time. You've got the makings of a perfect storm," he said.

30 [...] Rosalea Hamilton, one of the campaigners for Advocates Network who organised slavery reparations protests in Jamaica, said there was currently a "heightened consciousness of the history", including "understanding of the legacies of colonialism today, economic, sociological, psychological". There was, she said, an increased awareness that this had led to trauma in the population that affected confidence levels, along with swathes of the population living in
35 "unhealthy, unsanitary, unsafe" conditions. Reid said the reparations movement had been "gathering significant steam" in part because of increased access to information about Jamaica's history that went beyond the school textbooks that had traditionally taught a British interpretation of history.

"The man on the street is demanding reparations as well, it's not just at the intellectual level.
40 That's when you know something is really gathering momentum, when it's spreading across a broad section of society. More people are recognising the horror of slavery and the atrocities that were committed and becoming aware of the impact that has on modern day life."

(605 words)   Source: *The Guardian*, 25 March 2022

to **be supposed to be** *sollen*

platinum jubilee *siebzigjähriges Jubiläum*

reparations *Entschädigung*

enduring *beständig*

fury *Zorn*

to **discourage sb from doing sth** *jdm von etw abraten*

dispute *Streitfall*

patron *Schirmherr/in*

to **urge sb to do sth** *jdn drängen etw zu tun*

presumptuous *überheblich*

to **gain** *etw gewinnen, erlangen*

to **gush** *schwärmen*

to **dazzle** *schillern*

to **dub sb/sth** *jdn/ etw nennen*

to **come off** *gelingen*

to **deem sth as** *etw für … halten*

regal *königlich*

publication *Veröffentlichung, Zeitung*

to **devote** *widmen*

considerable *erheblich*

column inches *Spaltengröße*

abhorrent *abscheulich*

to **stage sth** *etw veranstalten*

makings *(hier:) Zutaten*

heightened *erhöht*

awareness *Bewusstsein*

trauma *seelische Erschütterung*

swathes *weite Teile*

unsanitary *unhygienisch*

to **gather steam** *Fahrt aufnehmen*

atrocity *Gräueltat*

to **commit sth** *etw begehen*

2 You can find the highlighted words from the text on page 61 in the table below.
Fill in the empty boxes in the following wordlist.

Word/Phrase	Memory support	German
_____ _____	**SENTENCE:** Although Prince Charles and Prince William have described slavery as an atrocity _____ against the people of Africa and of former colonies, no royal has ever said sorry.	etw begehen
confidence	**WORD FAMILY** _____ (v) confidence (n) _____ (adj) _____ (adv)	Vertrauen
_____	**COLLOCATIONS** ~ access, an advantage, control, independence, the impression that, an insight into sth, power, recognition, a reputation, sth by doing sth, sympathy	etw gewinnen, erlangen
publication	**WORD FAMILY** _____ (v) publication (n) _____ (n) _____ (adj) _____ (adj) _____ (adj) _____ (adv)	Veröffentlichung, Zeitung
_____	**SYNONYMS:** amends, compensation, redress	Entschädigung
racial	**WORD FAMILY** _____ (n) _____ (n) racial (adj) _____ (adj) _____ (adv)	rassisch, rassen-

3 'Platinum' is pronounced ˈplætɪnəm with a stress on the first syllable, like a lot of English words.
We can represent the stress pattern as ● • •. Dictionaries show the stress with this symbol ˈ.
Join the words from 'Words in context' with the correct stress pattern. A dictionary can help.

campaigner	• ●
monarchy	● • •
presumptuous	● • •
(to) present	• • ● •
reparations	• ● •
scandal	• ● • •

4 Use the words below to complete the collocations in 1–4. Put the verbs in the correct form.

average person • broad • (to) gather • protest • society • (to) stage • steam • street

1 In Germany, if you asked the _____ on the _____ about German colonial history, they wouldn't know very much.

2 Across Europe, the campaign to return museum artefacts taken from former colonies has been _____ _____.

3 There is support from a _____ section of _____ for the removal of the names of people associated with colonial history from streets and public places.

4 Descendants of former slaves _____ a _____ along the route of the Royals' visit to Kingston, Jamaica.

The chill out zone

1 True or false?

Take the quiz on the UK. Are these statements true or false? If you answer correctly, the letters under your answers will spell out something that represents the UK.

		True	False
1	In early English, **you** was the formal form of address, similar to *Sie* in German. **Thou** was the informal form of address, similar to *du*. But over time, English-speakers stopped using thou, leaving you as the only form.	□ U	□ T
2	The national day of the United Kingdom is November 5th, also known as Guy Fawkes' Day, and the British light large fires to celebrate their victory over the French in 1066 AD.	□ H	□ N
3	The only remaining copy of the British constitution is actually kept in a picture frame in the White House in Washington, D.C. It was captured by the Americans during their War of Independence.	□ E	□ I
4	The United Kingdom in its modern form dates only from 1922, when the southern part of Ireland gained its independence and the UK became the United Kingdom of Great Britain and Northern Ireland.	□ O	□ F
5	The five most important native languages of the UK are English, Scottish Gaelic, Welsh, Geordie and Irish Gaelic.	□ L	□ N
6	Because of anti-German feeling during World War 1, the British king, George V, changed the royal family's name from Saxe-Coburg-Gotha to Windsor.	□ J	□ A
7	India and Poland are the countries of birth of the two largest immigrant populations in the UK, with a combined resident population of 1.5 million.	□ A	□ P
8	One of London's most famous landmarks is Big Ben, the clock tower of the Houses of Parliament.	□ P	□ C
9	The flag of the United Kingdom is actually a combination of three flags: the flags of St Patrick, St George and St Andrew.	□ K	□ Y

Something that represents the UK? The ___ ___ ___ ___ ___ ___ ___ ___ ___.

2 UK geography

Label the maps A–F with the correct name from the box. There is one name you do not need.

England • Great Britain • Northern Ireland • Scotland • the British Isles • the United Kingdom • Wales

A _____

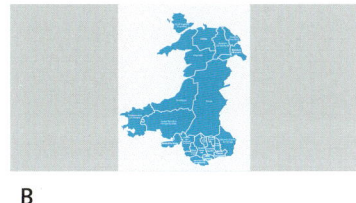

B _____

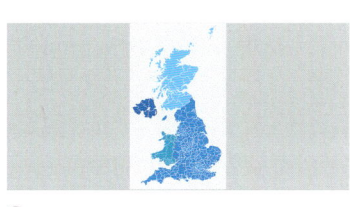

C _____

D _____

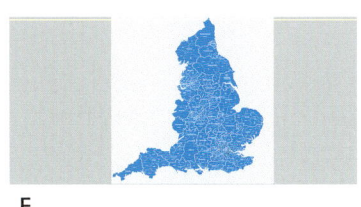

E _____

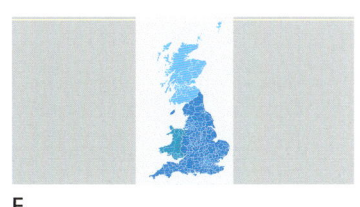

F _____

Getting to grips with grammar
p. 64 Do after Sections A & F

Dealing with visual material
p. 66 Do after Section F

Writing workshop 1
p. 68 Do after Section E

Dealing with listening tasks
p. 72 Do after Sections B, C or D

Writing workshop 2
p. 70 Do after the whole topic

Words in context
p. 73

The chill out zone
p. 75

Getting to grips with grammar

Do after any section

G ▸ *The present and past progressive, SB, pp. 283–284*

1 Simple or progressive verb forms

Look at the 16 verbs in the box. Write them into the correct part of the table below.
For the verbs that can normally be used in the progressive form, write in the progressive form.

be • become • cry • decide • die • doubt • have (*haben, besitzen*) • imagine • know • love • plan • prefer • rise • stand • travel • understand

Not usually used in the progressive form Verb	Progressive form can be used normally Verb	progressive form
be	become	becoming

Do after Section A

2 The simple past or past progressive

G ▶ *The past progressive, SB, p. 284*

Put in the correct form of the verb: the simple past or past progressive

The families of the Little Rock Nine *prepared*_____ (**prepare**) their children to expect trouble on the first day at Central High School. Despite being prepared, Elizabeth 1. _____ (**be**) shocked to see that a huge crowd of white adults and students, even soldiers, 2. _____ (**wait**) for her at the school. Elizabeth 3. _____ (**try**) to walk through the crowd, but the soldiers who 4. _____ (**stand**) in front of her 5. _____ (**raise**) their weapons. While Elizabeth 6. _____ (**search**) for a way into the school, the crowd 7. _____ (**scream**) and even 8. _____ (**spat**) at her. Another fifteen-year-old, white student Hazel Bryan, 9. _____ (**follow**) Elizabeth as she 10. _____ (**walk**) towards the school, screaming "Go back to Africa!" at the black girl. Elizabeth 11. _____ (**can**) see that the soldiers 12. _____ (**do**) nothing to protect her. In the end, she 13. _____ (**have to**) turn back because the situation 14. _____ (**become**) more and more violent and dangerous. It 15. _____ (**be**) the safest thing to do – the crowd even 16. _____ (**attack**) three Black journalists who 17. _____ (**take**) photographs. It 18. _____ (**take**) another three weeks before Elizabeth, Minnijean Brown-Trickey and the other seven black students 19. _____ (**manage**) to enter the high school.

Do after Section F

3 The present perfect: simple or progressive

G ▶ *The present perfect, present perfect progressive, SB, pp. 284–285*

Use the present perfect – in its simple or progressive form – and the highlighted words to express the meaning of the sentence pairs in one sentence. The first has been done as an example.

1 **Nazeem uses a wheelchair**. He got his first wheelchair when **he was two years old**.

   *Nazeem has been using a wheelchair since he was two years old.*_____

2 **Nazeem loves fashion**. When **he was a young child**, he loved fashion.

   _____

3 **He goes to fashion shows** regularly. The first show he went to was in **2010.**

   _____

4 A fashion magazine **published Nazeem's** first article in **2020**. Then other **fashion magazines** published two more **articles** last year.

   _____

5 **Nazeem is writing a new article** at the moment. He started writing the article **two hours** ago.

   _____

6 **He is** also **searching for an internship in fashion publishing**. He began his search **two weeks** ago.

   _____

Dealing with visual material

Do after Section F

1 a Describing images: Use the words from the table below to describe the locations of the letters in the image. You can use the words as many times as you need but use every word at least once. Write in your exercise book.

in on at	the	left lower right top upper background bottom centre corner foreground

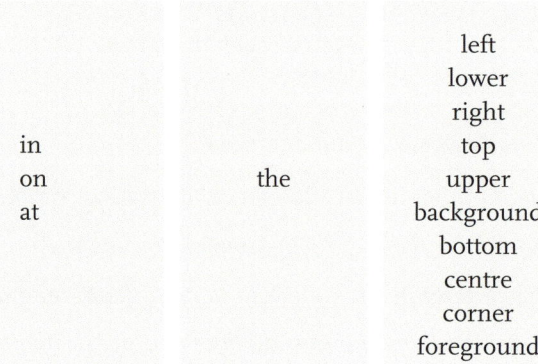

b Now use some of the phrases from exercise 1a) to write a description of the image. You can find the image without labels on page 240 of your student's book. You can use the vocabulary in the box.

> a female (religious / humanist) minister • to perform a (same-sex / gay) wedding ceremony • to hold hands • grooms (*Bräutigame*) • to marry / get married • lawn / grass • bushes / shrubs / shrubbery

2 Describing images: Write in the correct adjectives to describe the shapes and objects in the pictures below.

> circular • cylindrical • irregular • jagged • oval • rectangular • square • triangular

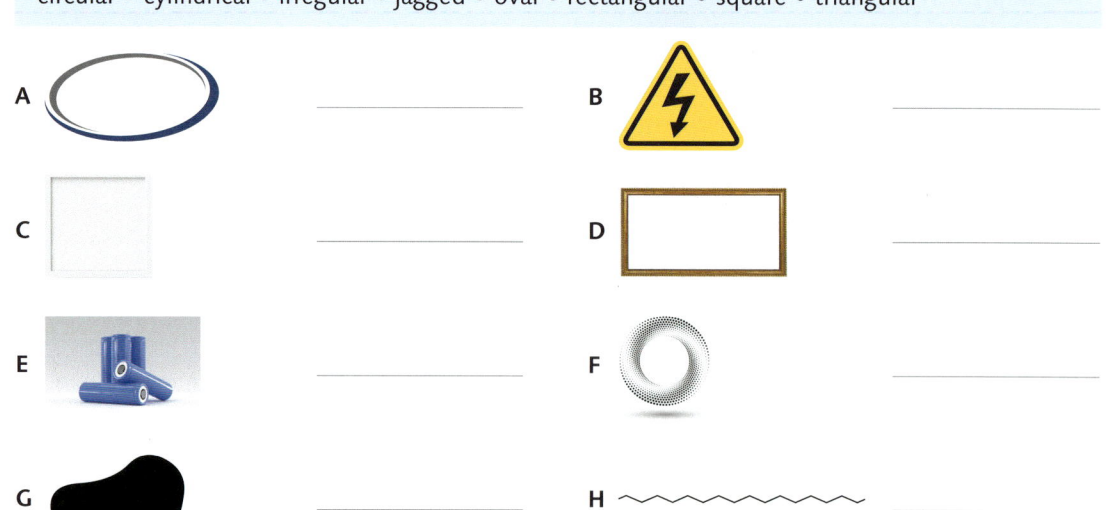

A _____

B _____

C _____

D _____

E _____

F _____

G _____

H _____

3 a Dealing with cartoons: Examine the cartoon for a minute. Note down your first reaction to it and what you think its message might be. Then do tasks b)-d).

Look at your student's book pages 82–83 and the PagePlayer App for more help.

b <u>Underline</u> the best alternative to complete the description of the cartoon above.

The black and white cartoon is <u>made up of</u> / made out of two horizontal stripes / strips. In the first frame, we see / are seeing two people, a man on the left and another person on the right. We can only see their heads and shoulders and it is difficult to tell / speak if the person on the right is a man or a woman. In the first three frames, the man is talking / talks to the other person and in the second and third frames we can the man only see / only see the man. From what the man is saying, it is clear that he is unsure / unsafe how to describe the other person without making / causing offence. He is wondering whether he should say 'disabled', 'handicapped' or perhaps 'differently abled'. In the fourth and final frame, the cartoon zooms out to reveal / uncover that the man is standing / stands and the other person is in fact a wheelchair user. Now we know this person is also / too a man and he responds to other man's questions by saying he prefers / favours to be called 'Mike'.

c Now use your notes from exercise 3a) to say what you think the message of the cartoon is. You might find it helpful to review the work you did in exercise 10 (the social barriers in particular) on page 252 of the student's book.

d Use your notes from 3a) again, but this time to evaluate the cartoon. Consider these questions in writing your answer:
- Do you believe the cartoon is effective or ineffective in conveying its message?
- What specific elements of the cartoon can you mention to support your opinion?
- What impact does the cartoon have on you?

How to say it or write it

I believe the point the cartoonist is making is … / The message of the cartoon is clearly …
The fact that we have to wait until later … is an (in)effective technique …
The cartoon made me reflect / stop and think …

Writing workshop 1

Do after Section E

Look at your student's book page 81 and the PagePlayer App for more help.

Writing a summary

1 Text function: Look at the title and skim the text on the next page. Tick the correct option.

The function of the text is …

☐ **a** to inform the reader about meritocracy and describe how it works.

☐ **b** to argue the pros and cons of meritocracy so that society adopts it.

☐ **c** to persuade the reader that meritocracy needs to be changed in some way.

Good to know

Being able to recognize the function, type and structure of a text is also important in a text analysis task.

2 Text type: Complete the introductory sentence with the correct word from (a–e) below.

a a report   **b** an editorial   **c** a feature   **d** a letter to the editor   **e** a comment

The article is _____ written by Nick Timothy and was published in *The Telegraph* newspaper on 6 June 2021.

3 Structure: Your summary should reflect the structure of the original text. Skim the article and decide which structure (a–e) matches the text most closely. If you are not sure, do exercise 4 first.

a description	**b** sequence and order	**c** comparisons and contrasts	**d** cause and effect	e problem and solution

4 Read lines 1–21 of the text carefully and write the letter (a, b or c) for the best description in the box on the right.

a The author believes that society rewards hard work less now than it did in the past. He compares Victorian times with the current situation and finds a contrast: society has become less meritocratic. The evidence which he presents to support this finding includes …

b The author lays out his belief that Britain faces a challenge in addressing inequality because meritocracy, the concept that society rewards somebody's hard work, by itself is not enough to help working-class people improve their situation. He supports his view by citing …

c In his article, the author focuses on a number of issues in British society today. He presents a number of causes for these. He links wealth inheritance with the rising number of people in a "low pay trap". He goes on to say that the negative attitude of the country's richest communities is one reason why the professions are out of reach for working-class people. He then describes …

5 The topic sentences in a text can help you identify important points that a good summary should contain. Look at the topic sentences from the text below and, in your exercise book, answer the question which follows each one. Write only one or two sentences.

l. 26 "Research from the United States certainly suggests that this is the case."

a What is "the case"?

l. 36 "This is the paradox of meritocracy."

b What is the "paradox of meritocracy"?

6 Now, using your work in exercises 1–5 as preparation, do the following task:

Summarize the author's view of social equality in Britain today and what improvements British society can make.

Opinion: Nick Timothy
Meritocracy remains our best option, but it cannot work without social solidarity

Who could disagree with meritocracy, the idea that our prospects should depend not on the circumstances of birth, but our talents and efforts alone?

The answer, it turns out, is rather a lot of people. [...] On the Left, it is attacked as elitist and a cover for "white privilege". On the Right, it is associated with the managerial elites who gave us
5 globalisation, mass immigration and membership of the European Union. [...]

A problem [...] is that our meritocracy is not [...] especially meritocratic. The Institute for Fiscal Studies says "inheritance is probably the most crucial factor in determining a person's wealth since Victorian times". The Sutton Trust, comparing the experiences of sons born in 1958 and in 1970, found that "in just one decade, Britain had become less (socially) mobile".

10 The Government's Social Mobility Commission agrees. Five million workers, mainly women, are "in a low pay trap from which few find escape". Only one in six who were low paid in 2006 had found a lasting route out of low pay a decade later. And wealth inequality is deep and growing deeper: the richest 10 per cent of households enjoy five times the accumulated wealth of the bottom half of all households combined.

15 At the top of the labour market, the professions remain beyond many working-class people. Only 6 per cent of doctors, 12 per cent of company chief executives, and 12 per cent of journalists come from working-class families. [...]

We sometimes hear about the poor academic performance of white working-class boys. Part of the likely explanation is that the best-performing schools in the country are in London, where only 10
20 per cent of the white population of England and Wales lives. By contrast, 36 per cent of Asians and 58 per cent of black people live in the capital.

Likewise, some of the country's richest communities [...] are among the worst places to live for disadvantaged students. But some of the country's poorest communities, such as Slough, are social mobility hotspots. This might be explained in part by the strong families and social
25 networks among the large Asian population there.

Research from the United States certainly suggests that this is the case. In his book, Fractured, the British author Jon Yates reveals that the one city in America with Scandinavian levels of social mobility is in the state that spends least on education. Perhaps surprisingly, it is largely white, votes Republican and is highly religious. It is Salt Lake City, and its success appears to be linked
30 to its social trust, with children from rich and poor families attending the same schools, visiting temple together, and forming the same social networks.

Academic studies confirm a strong correlation between high social mobility and strong social trust, in the form of membership associations and clubs and an absence of racial and economic division. These factors have a correlation with social mobility stronger even than education
35 spending, the quality of university education, and the local employment rate.

This is the paradox of meritocracy. If we want all our citizens to have the chance to achieve their true potential, and if we want to make sure that jobs go to the people best equipped to do them, we have to think beyond meritocracy itself: we must aim to restore a sense of the common good. [...]

40 By restoring social capital, focusing on community, and embracing our need to belong, government motivated by the common good can create the conditions in which individuals are best able to achieve their potential. Doing so would also avoid the worst excesses of meritocratic culture. Instead of believing that the winner takes all, the successful should remember the people and places, the communities and institutions, to whom they owe their success. [...]

45 For we are all standing on the shoulders of somebody. If we do believe in rewarding merit, if we want more individuals to succeed, we need to do more, together, to lift everyone up.

(660 words)   Source: *The Telegraph*, 6 June 2021

Writing workshop 2

Do after you have finished the whole topic

Look at your student's book pages 126–128 and the PagePlayer App for more help.

Dealing with a creative writing task

Creative writing tasks can be related to an overall theme or subject, and not just a specific text. To complete the task, you may be expected to rely on your own knowledge of the theme.

1 Look at the example task in a) below. Then make a table in your exercise book like b). Go back through Topic 6, collect ideas and information that will help you to do the writing task and add them to your table. You may also include information you have learned from other classwork.

a "If you are a woman, a member of a minority or a person with a disability, the world is still a very unequal place."
Write an article for your school magazine, commenting on the quotation.

b

Ideas and information from Topic 6 and other classwork		
Section	Agreeing with the quotation	Disagreeing with the quotation
A	• Despite all the progress, people in the US still have to protest and fight for equal civil rights, e.g. the killing of George Floyd "felt like the 1960s, even worse because it was 50 years later [and] it's still not a better time" (SB, p. 229, ll. 55–56) • In class, we learned about actions (voter ID laws) in the US which make voting more difficult for minorities	• The timeline of civil rights in the US shows concrete progress, e.g. elections of Barack Obama as president and Kamala Harris as vice president; the worldwide attention and outrage against mistreatment of Black people (SB, pp. 226–227) • Minnijean Brown-Trickey of the Little Rock Nine is "far from drowning in despair. She is very proud of the way young people are taking up the fight for racial justice" (SB, p. 229, ll. 65–66) • In our social studies class, we learned about the laws against discrimination in Germany and very many other countries ….
B	• Women make up only a quarter of representatives in parliaments around the world (SB, p. 281)	• Women's participation in parliaments around the world has doubled in the last 25 years (SB, p. 281)

2 a Imagine a classmate asks you to check the first draft of their comment for the task in exercise 1a).
You find some mistakes but are not sure how to describe them. Match the labels below with the sections 1–7 of the text containing the issue on the next page. The first (A) has been done for you, but the others are not in chronological order.

A Text type – wrong type of text/audience   B Vocabulary – German influence

C Grammar – wrong tense   D Style – German sentence structure

E Vocabulary – repetitive use of same   F Structure – separate paragraphs
  expression   needed for different ideas

G Style – mix of formal and informal style

EXAMPLE FROM TEXT	Issue:

1 Ladies and gentlemen, I am here today to talk to you about inequality, namely the idea that the world is still a very unequal place if you are a woman, a member of a minority or a person with a disability. I would like to begin my talk by being open about the fact that I am male, not a member of a minority group and I do not have a mental or physical disability. Nevertheless, while I do not believe the sentiment expressed by the quotation is completely wrong, I feel it is an unhelpfully negative approach to the topic. In this speech, I hope to explain why I feel there are more reasons to be positive about the issue of equality than reasons to be negative.

A

2 Yeah, I will admit the world is far from perfect, but you gotta say that we've made a heck of a lot of progress, especially in the last few years. We have to focus on the positive, not the negative. I will illustrate my point with some examples.

___

3 In the USA, within the last 15 years we have witnessed the first Black president and the first Black vice president. Of course, racism and mistreatment are still problems, but the US today is a far more equal country than it was in the Jim Crow era and the time of the Little Rock Nine when people of colour were officially second-class citizens in many states. Now, let me move on to gender equality. As I said before, the world in terms of women's equality is not ideal, but again, improvements have been made.

___

4 The representation of women in parliaments of countries around the world over the last twenty-five years has doubled.

___

5   Admittedly, this increase is bringing the percentage of women parliamentarians to a still unsatisfactory 25%, nevertheless it shows we move in the right direction.

___

6 For sexual and gender minorities, until 2001 not one country on the entire planet recognized the right of a person – man or woman – to be married with somebody of the same gender, but today gay marriage is legal in 24 countries and accepted in 27 more. Surely this is a ground for optimism.

___

7 If you are a person with a disability, I think the world today is a lot better than it was. I think advances in technology and changes in people's attitudes have gone hand in hand. Cities such as Seattle in the USA or Melbourne, Australia, are leading the way in making the urban environment more accessible through better design and the use of technology. I think the fact that people are more aware of conditions such as ADHD or Asperger's Syndrome is a healthy sign of society becoming more inclusive.

___

b In your exercise book, rewrite the parts of sections 1–7 correcting the issues you identified. The first has been done for you.

A I would like to begin this article about the quotation in the title by being open about the fact that I am male, not a member of a minority group and I do not have a mental or physical disability. Nevertheless, while I do not believe the sentiment expressed by the quotation is completely wrong, I feel it is an unhelpfully negative approach to the topic. In my article, I hope to explain why I feel there are more reasons to be positive about the issue of equality than reasons to be negative.

3 Now, using the information you gathered in 1b), do exercise 1a) yourself. When you have finished, check your text to avoid any of the issues from exercise 2a).

Dealing with listening tasks

Do after Sections B, C or D

Look at your student's book pages 123–125 and the PagePlayer App for more help.

Equality

Task type: short answers

1 If you don't know how to pronounce English words, you may have difficulty recognizing them in a listening text. The words below are very important for the theme of equality, so it is important to know how they are pronounced.

   a Look up the words in a dictionary, read the phonetic transcription and practise pronouncing them.
   Example: bias *(noun)* /ˈbaɪəs/

> bias • discrimination • diversity • ethnic • harassment • inclusivity • LGBTQ •
> minority • prejudice • racist

🔊 08
   b Now listen carefully and circle five words from a) which you hear. Be careful – there are three words which are not from a).

🔊 09 2 Now it is time to do the listening task.

   You will hear an interview about equality in the UK. While listening, take notes on the following points. You need not write complete sentences.
   You now have time to read the assignment.

   1 What proportion of workers polled experienced discrimination or were treated badly because of their identity?

   • _____

   2 What were the consequences of this discrimination? (3 aspects)

   • _____

   • _____

   • _____

   3 What change to the law do some black workers feel the UK should make?

   • _____

   4 What can be said about the gender pay gap for women with immigrant backgrounds? (2 aspects)

   • _____

   • _____

   5 What positives in terms of equality are mentioned? (2 aspects)

   • _____

   • _____

   6 What should be done to make society more equal? (2 aspects)

   • _____

   • _____

Words in context

1 Read the newspaper comment on the attitudes towards transgender people in the UK.

Forget toxic Twitter debates: the UK isn't as divided on trans rights as you think

For a country famed for its modesty and reserve, the UK does seem to have found itself having an awful lot of conversations about genitalia before breakfast. I'm talking, of course, about the [...] increasingly acrimonious row about trans rights.

[...] But having spent many evenings over the past few months talking to ordinary Britons across
5 the country from Glasgow to Witney and Brighton to Blyth (along with polling of 5,000 others), we found the public talked about trans people [...] in a way that was totally removed from the debate playing out on the airwaves or our phone screens.

Log on to Twitter and it appears as though Britain is divided in two: between the trans allies and the transphobes. But when you log off and swap 280 characters for proper conversations, you see
10 a very different picture.

First, most people start from a position of compassion about the struggles that trans people face. Many people shared stories with us about their trans colleagues, students, friends and family, with roughly a quarter of the population knowing someone who is trans according to our research. They shared respect for people's bravery and gratitude that things had got better in recent
15 years, along with frustration about the challenges and discrimination that trans people still face.

Most Britons don't think the debate about trans people is one of the most important issues facing our country today (in fact, according to our research, only 2% do). [...] But that doesn't mean the public aren't informed about the issues involved – in fact, we heard plenty of stories about the common-sense approaches that they've taken to accommodating trans people in their schools,
20 communities and workplaces.

Almost no one we spoke to got worked up about calling someone by their preferred pronouns. Most thought it was important that schools were making trans pupils feel supported and were also teaching young people that trans people existed. Some found the new terminology they heard from their children confusing, but their concerns were about being shouted at for getting things
25 wrong or asking questions rather than hostility to change.

Instead, by and large, the public take a "live and let live approach" as long as it doesn't undermine notions of fairness and fair play. That explains, for instance, why most people were happy, or indifferent, to the idea of introducing more unisex toilets [...]

However, they were opposed (57% to 19%) to allowing trans women to compete in women's
30 sports – not because they want to police who does and who doesn't count as a woman, but because they don't think it's fair. [...] (M)ost teachers in our focus groups said it was important that they respected children as they explored their gender identity. But at the same time people didn't want children to undergo irreversible processes – such as taking cross-sex hormones – before the age of 18 or without proper medical advice and support. Far from two binary positions, the Britons we
35 spoke to constantly strove to find the fairest path forward – embracing trans inclusion on some issues and wanting to preserve sex-based boundaries on others.

It was also clear that most people don't see trans people as one monolithic group – they distinguished between those who had been through gender reassignment surgery and those who hadn't, or those who had lived in their expressed gender for a long time and those for a short time.
40 They felt that it was important to take a case-by-case approach [...]

More than anything, the public wanted the space to be able to talk about these issues and to try to find a way through. The greatest threat to that is if the toxic discourse starts to bleed into the public conversation, leaving people afraid of being shouted down or labelled as bigots. Such an outcome would be bad for trans people, bad for those concerned about the protection of sex-based
45 rights, and bad for society at large as we grapple with how to handle issues of social change.

(680 words)   Source: *The Guardian*, 16 June 2022

famed *berühmt*
modesty *Bescheidenheit*
reserve *Zurückhaltung*
acrimonious *bitter*
row *Streit*
to poll *jdn befragen*
(far) removed from sth *weit entfernt von etw*
to play out *sich abspielen*
to be on the airwaves *gesendet werden*
to swap *tauschen*
compassion *Mitgefühl*
to face sth *etw begegnen*
roughly *ungefähr*
bravery *Mut*
gratitude *Dankbarkeit*
common sense *Alltagsdenken*
approach *Herangehensweise, Ansatz*
to accommodate sb *jdm entgegenkommen*
to get worked up about sth *sich über etw aufregen*
preferred *bevorzugt*
terminology *Begrifflichkeiten*
confusing *verwirrend*
by and large *im Großen und Ganzen*
indifferent *gleichgültig*
to police sth/sb *jdn/etw kontrollieren*
to undergo sth *etw durchmachen*
to strive *anstreben*
inclusion *Eingliederung*
boundary *Abgrenzung*
gender reassignment surgery *geschlechtsanglei-chende Operation*
expressed *zum Ausdruck gebracht, entfaltet*
discourse *Diskurs*
to bleed into sth *etw vergiften*
bigot *Fanatiker/in*
outcome *Ergebnis*
at large *im Allgemeinen*
to grapple with sth *mit etw kämpfen*

2   You can find the highlighted words from the text on page 73 in the table below.
Fill in the empty boxes in the following wordlist.

Word/Phrase	Memory support	German
_____	**COLLOCATIONS** to ~ a challenge, discrimination, hostility, an issue, opposition, a problem, the possibility of sth, a struggle, a threat	etwas begegnen
_____	**SENTENCE:** If everyone had more _____ for the problems of others, the world would be a better place.	Mitgefühl
expressed	**WORD FAMILY** _____ (vb) _____ (n) expressed (adj) _____ (adj) _____ (adv)	zum Ausdruck gebracht, entfaltet
_____	**WORD FAMILY** to include sth / sb (vb) _____ (n) _____ (n) _____ (adj)	Eingliederung
roughly	**SYNONYMS:** _____	ungefähr
supported	**WORD FAMILY** _____ (vb) _____ (n) _____ (n) supported (adj) _____ (adj)	unterstützt

3   **a**   The word *row* in line 3 of the text is a homograph, one of two or more words that are spelled the same but do not have the same pronunciation or meaning. Match the phonetic transcriptions (a, b) of the two versions of *row* with the correct meaning (1, 2).

   a [rəʊ]   **1** a serious argument between people, organizations, etc. about something
   b [raʊ]   **2** a number of people, objects, words or numbers next to each other in a line

   b   Using a monolingual dictionary, write out the different meanings of these homographs.

> bow • content • frequent • minute • second • tear • wind

4   Complete the collocations taken from 'Words in context' with the correct preposition from the list. There is one more than you need.

> about • between • for • from • over • with

   1 The Californian city of San Francisco is famed _____ being LGBTQ+-friendly.

   2 With the legalisation of gay marriage in 2015 and a gay prime minister, Ireland today is far
removed _____ its history as a conservative, Roman Catholic country.

   3 People who are against equal rights for LGBTQ+ often use extreme examples just to get people
worked up _____ the issue.

   4 A fair society would not distinguish _____ people when it comes to human rights.

   5 If you are grappling _____ issues around LGBTQ+, just ask yourself how would you
like people to treat your friend or family member if they were gay or transgender?

The chill out zone

1 A multi-culti world

We sometimes think certain things are traditionally German, really British or very American, but are they? Complete these sentences with the letter (A–E) of the correct country of origin.

A China B France C Germany D Iran E Ireland

1 Beer! What could be more German? But beer was first produced 7,000 years ago in … .   _____

2 Because of American TV and movies, many people think Halloween is an American tradition, but actually the tradition was brought to the US by immigrants from … .   _____

3 Italy is famous for its delicious ice cream and love of coffee. Most people know that coffee first came from the Middle East, but not many people know that Marco Polo brought the idea of ice cream to Italy after visiting … .   _____

4 If you think of the Netherlands, do you think of tulips, windmills and bicycles? Well, tulips and windmills came to Europe from the Asia and the Middle East while the inventor of the first bicycle was from … .   _____

5 Jeans seem as American as apple pie, but the material, denim, that jeans are made of was actually invented in the 18th century in … .   _____

2 Inclusive language

Words have power – the power to make people feel empowered and respected. Complete these tips with the right words from the box.

> attendant • condition • heritage • lives • native speaker • people • stereotypes • they • unique

Culture	• _____ of nationalities are usually wrong and often offensive. Don't let them influence your opinions and don't share them. • Don't make the mistake of thinking that using English swear / curse words will make you sound more like a _____ – it won't. Some curse words are discriminatory and no longer used today.
Gender and sexuality	• Use more gender-neutral words. For example, you can say '_____' instead of 'waiter / waitress' or 'flight steward / stewardess', or 'businessperson' instead of 'businessman / businesswoman'. • In English, we often use the pronoun '_____' to refer to one person when the gender is unknown or unimportant, e.g. an unknown author. Some members of the LGBTQ+ community prefer people to use it to refer to them as individuals instead of the gendered pronouns he or she.
Physical and health matters	• We are _____ first – remember that. Say 'people with a disability' or 'people with visual impairment' rather than 'the disabled' or 'the blind'. • Don't describe people with mental illness or a psychiatric _____ as 'crazy' or 'mad'. Say a person has or _____ with cancer, for example, instead of 'suffers from' cancer.
Race	• Some people with African _____ prefer black (or Black) while some prefer 'person of colour'. It is unacceptable to say 'coloured'. Some people whose parents are different races use the term 'mixed race' to describe themselves while some say 'biracial'.
General	• Avoid phrases like 'normal people'. There is no such thing as 'normal' – we are all different and _____ in interesting ways.

Key features of the Listening Section

- Exam time: 30 minutes
- Audio recordings: between 2–3 minutes each
- You have time before the audio to read the tasks.
- You hear each recording twice.
- You have a short time after the second listening to work on your answers.
- Marks: 20% of total exam
- Task types: three tasks → multiple choice, multiple matching, short answers or sentence completion

Steps for task 1 (multiple matching)

Step 1: Notice key words in the task description e.g. genetically modified (GM) food.

Step 2: Read the task *carefully*. Only use a dictionary to look up words you really don't know.

Step 3: Brainstorm key vocabulary related to the topic and possible synonyms for key words / phrases.

Step 4: Listen to the recording the first time. Don't panic if you don't understand everything.

Step 5: Lightly mark the answers you are sure of in the first listening.

Step 6: During the second listening, concentrate on the answers you don't have. Lightly mark them.

Step 7: After the second listening, review your answers. Write **one** answer for each *clearly*.

If any answers are missing, make a good guess – what sounds most logical given what you heard?

Steps for task 2 (short answers)

Step 1: Notice key words in the task description, e.g. the Windrush generation.

Step 2: Read the task *carefully*. Only use a dictionary to look up words you really don't know.

Step 3: Brainstorm key vocabulary related to the topic and possible synonyms for key words / phrases in the opinions.

Step 4: Listen to the recording the first time. Make short notes on a sheet of paper.

Step 5: During the second listening, concentrate on the answers you don't have.

Step 6: After the second listening, review your answers. Do not give more answers than each question asks for, e.g. name **two** aspects. If no number is given, only one answer is needed. You can write figures as numbers, not words, e.g. 5,000 *not* five thousand.

Step 7: If any answers are missing, make a good guess – what sounds most logical given what you heard?

Aufgabenteil I   Hören

Task 1: GM food

You will hear five people talking about genetically modified (GM) food. While listening, match the opinions A to G with speakers 1 to 5. There are two more opinions than you need.

You now have time to read the assignment.

Opinion	
A	GM food tastes horrible.
B	Have faith in modern technology.
C	GM food allows big business to exploit farmers.
D	This experimentation is putting our own existence at risk.
E	Unmodified food is already abundant – GM food is unnecessary.
F	After altering our environment so much already, there's no point fretting now.
G	Human intelligence is natural evolution and so is the technology humans invent.

Speaker	1	2	3	4	5
Heading					

Now listen to the recording again.

Task 2: The UK and the Windrush generation

You will hear a successful British Jamaican comedian, Kingsley Jones, talking about his experience as a child of Jamaican immigrants to the UK in the 1960s.

While listening, take notes on the following points. You need not write complete sentences. Now you have time to read the assignment.

1. What advice did Kingsley's mother give him and his siblings? Name three aspects.
2. What price did following the advice have for Kingsley?
3. What did Kingsley's mother herself do with the advice?
4. After his research, what did Kingsley understand about the Windrush generation? Name two aspects.
5. What conclusion did Kingsley draw about Jamaican culture when he was a teenager?

6 What does he think now about the jokes he performed at the beginning of his career?

7 What did he decide to do in order to be successful in British mainstream culture? Name three aspects.

Now listen to the recording again.

Task 3: The gig economy

You will hear an interview with Tom, a worker in the gig economy. While listening, answer (a, b or c) for each question. There is only one correct answer.

1 Tom describes the traditional American Dream as …
a taking every opportunity you can before you are old and grey. ☐
b a wheel which goes around and rewards people by chance. ☐
c doing the same thing again and again and only enjoying life when you are old. ☐

2 The global financial crisis was a positive event for Tom because …
a his old job was so interesting, he might have stayed there forever. ☐
b losing his job forced him to re-evaluate his life and become more inventive. ☐
c deciding to quit his comfortable job made him see other options were possible. ☐

3 Tom rediscovered his love for creative work …
a after a lot of careful consideration. ☐
b after attending many unsuccessful job interviews. ☐
c after realizing that he had never really been interested in architecture. ☐

4 Tom's creative activity expanded to become a kind of art school, but …
a it was never very successful. ☐
b its success meant he felt trapped by it. ☐
c it was so successful that it made him ill. ☐

5 Tom thinks that a job that provides short-term contracts …
a enables him to do the work he really loves. ☐
b cannot be combined with other types of work. ☐
c means more flexibility for people with different ways of life. ☐

6 All in all, Tom thinks that working as a gig worker …
a the drawbacks outweigh the benefits. ☐
b the benefits outweigh the drawbacks. ☐
c means he is able to take time to take care of himself. ☐

Now listen to the recording again.

Steps for task 3 (multiple matching)

Step 1: Notice key words in the task description e.g. gig economy.

Step 2: Read the task *carefully*. Only use a dictionary to look up words you really don't know.

Step 3: Brainstorm key vocabulary related to the topic and possible synonyms for key words/phrases in the opinions.

Step 4: Listen to the recording the first time. Don't panic if you don't understand everything.

Step 5: Lightly mark answers you are sure of in the first listening.

Step 6: During the second listening, concentrate on the answers you don't have. Lightly mark them.

Step 7: After the second listening, review your answers. Mark only **one** box.

If any answers are missing, make your best guess – what sounds most logical given what you heard?

- Exam time: 195 minutes
- Exam start: 10 minutes after the Listening Section
- Tasks: You will have two sets of tasks and you must choose **one set** to work on.
- Marks: 55% of total exam
- Each set has three tasks:
  - **Task 1:** Write a guided summary of a non-literary text. Source text will be 600–800 words long.
  - **Task 2:** Text analysis involves examining language, structure and stylistic means used by the author.
  - **Task 3:** You will have a choice between an argumentative / evaluative writing task or a creative writing task for a specific purpose and audience.
    One assignment will relate closely to the text, while the other will relate to the general theme in question. For this, you might need to use your wider knowledge. Extra material may also be given, e.g. graphics, quotes, cartoons, etc.

Aufgabenteil II   Lesen und Schreiben

Aufgabenstellung

1 State the author's view on society's current approach to climate change and describe his proposed solution.

2 Analyse how the author tries to convince the reader of his position. Refer to language and stylistic devices.

3 Choose <u>one</u> of the following:

A "The main cause of your environmental impact isn't your attitude [...] It's your money."

Assess this statement considering the information given in the diagram (on page 80) and the text.

B Write a letter to the editor of the newspaper which published the text "Capitalism is killing the planet …" setting out your views on how consumer culture must change in the era of climate change.

---

1 State the author's view on society's current approach to climate change and describe his proposed solution.

Task 1 – Understanding the assignment	Task 1 – Doing the assignment
• Read the assignment carefully. What exactly should you summarize? • Typical instructions focus on specific aspects of the text contents: *Summarize* <u>what the author says about</u> … *Outline* <u>the effects</u> of … as mentioned in … *Point out* <u>the reason(s)</u> … *Describe* the author's experience … *State* the author's opinion on … and *Illustrate* with examples … • Read the text carefully and highlight <u>only the parts relevant to the assignment</u>.	• Plan and structure what you want to write: introduction → main part → conclusion. • Plan paragraphs for separate ideas. • Use the simple present. • Begin by describing the text type and giving details such as the author, where the text is taken from, etc. • Use <u>your own words</u> to paraphrase what you highlighted. • Only use direct quotations if the assignment asks you to illustrate with examples from the text.

2 Analyse how the author tries to convince the reader of his position. Refer to language and stylistic devices.

Task 2 – Understanding the assignment

- Read the task carefully. What exactly should you analyse or examine? The task may ask for a general analysis or it may ask you to focus in particular on language, structure and / or graphics, photos, cartoons, etc.
- Always ask yourself *"What effect does the author want to have on the reader?"* when analysing the text.

- **Linguistic or rhetorical means** can include:
  - **register** – formal, neutral or informal. Consider also choice of vocabulary, e.g. specialist or technical terms, colloquial or slang phrases, etc.
  - **tone** – a text may be written in one tone throughout or it may change, e.g. an author may first employ humour to engage readers but then adopt an urgent tone to warn and appeal for action.
  - **stylistic devices** – you are expected to recognize and name the literary devices used (e.g. alliteration, repetition, metaphors, etc.) and the effect they have on readers.
  - **type of argument** – if the text seeks to convince or persuade readers of a position, what type of argument does the author use? Types include practical, normative or indirect argument, argument by authority, or by analogy.

- **Structural means** can include:
  - **overall text structure** – how does the author open their text? Why? E.g. an interesting or funny anecdote engages readers quickly. How is the main part structured to build an argument or maintain reader interest? How does the author close the text? Why? E.g. supplying an answer to a question posed at the beginning may wrap up a text in a satisfying way for the reader.
  - **structure in detail** – how does the way the author structures and presents information or arguments help them achieve their goal? The information may be presented chronologically (clear and easy to follow); the author may describe a problem and then a solution (engaging); they may employ comparisons and contrast (impact).

Task 2 – Doing the assignment

- Read the text carefully. Highlight the features relevant to your analysis.
- Plan and structure what you want to write – introduction → main part → conclusion.
- Write in a neutral style. Do not make positive / negative judgements and do not give your opinion on the topic.
- Your introduction should contain information on the text source, author and the author's intention.
- Plan paragraphs for different aspects of the analysis.
- Your main part should support your statement in the introduction about the purpose of the text.
- Do not only write a list of stylistic devices, etc. Explain the effect the author achieves by using them.
- Your conclusion should refer back to your introduction and express the main point of your analysis in one sentence using different words. Add no new information.

3 Choose <u>one</u> of the following:

A "The main cause of your environmental impact isn't your attitude […] It's your money."

Assess this statement considering the information given in the graph and the text.

B Write a letter to the editor of the newspaper which published the text "Capitalism is killing the planet …" setting out your views on how consumer culture must change in the era of climate change.

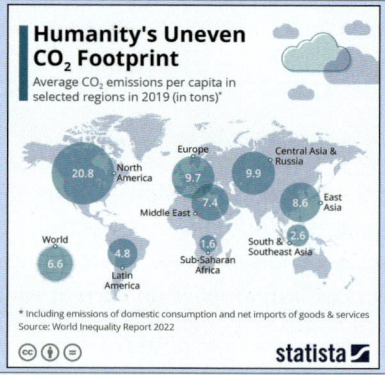

Humanity's Uneven CO₂ Footprint
Average CO_2 emissions per capita in selected regions in 2019 (in tons)*

* Including emissions of domestic consumption and net imports of goods & services
Source: World Inequality Report 2022

statista

Task 3 – Understanding the assignments

- One of the assignments will relate closely to the text, while the other will relate to the general theme in question. For the more general assignment, you might need to use your wider knowledge. Extra material may also be given for the assignments, e.g. graphics, quotes, cartoons, etc.
- The first task is an argumentative writing task where you are asked to assess, comment or discuss an aspect related to the text or the wider theme the text touches on.
- The second task is more creative and can take the form of an email, a letter, blog entry, speech, newspaper / website article, a dialogue or an inner monologue. As well as a defined format, the text will have a purpose and defined audience / reader(s).

Argumentative writing task

- Read the assignment carefully. The key verbs will help you to know what is expected:
  - Comment on / Give your opinion – you should present your opinion using arguments and examples
  - Assess / Evaluate / Discuss / Weigh up the pros and cons. You should reach a carefully considered conclusion after examining a complex topic from different viewpoints.

Creative writing task

- Read the assignment carefully. Identify what text type, purpose and target audience are required.
- Text type – some formats are looser, but some have features you must include, e.g. emails / letters (Dear Sir / Madam, … Yours faithfully), speech (Ladies and Gentlemen, … call to action), blog (informal style).
- Purpose – this can involve commenting on an issue or assessing, evaluating, etc. so you need to follow the same principles as given in the section above.

Task 3 – Doing the assignment

- Consider the task carefully. Does it relate to the text and specific materials or do you need to use your wider knowledge of the theme?
- Brainstorm ideas. Use an organizer to visualize connections between aspects: mind map, fishbone or Venn diagram, flow chart.
- Plan and structure what you want to write – introduction → main part → conclusion.
- Plan paragraphs for different aspects of your text. Argumentative texts can use an hourglass or a zigzag structure.
- Begin paragraphs using topic sentences and make your writing coherent by using connectives to link your ideas.
- Think of your text as building towards the end. Begin with your weakest points / arguments and finish with your strongest.
- Always keep in mind the task type. A creative task such as a speech often involves stating your position at the beginning, while an argumentative task usually requires you to stay objective until your final paragraph.
- The final paragraph of an argumentative text is where you draw conclusions on what you have written. This might be from a *for* or an *against* stance, or you might prefer to come to a compromise. The one thing you must do, though, is <u>adopt a clear position</u>.

Capitalism is killing the planet – it's time to stop buying into our own destruction
by George Monbiot

There is a myth about human beings that withstands all evidence. It's that we always put our survival first. This is true of other species. [...] Humans are a different matter.

When faced with an impending or chronic threat, such as climate or ecological breakdown, we seem to go out of our way to compromise our survival. We convince ourselves that it's not so serious, or even that it isn't happening. [...]

Human civilisation relies on current equilibrium states. But, all over the world, crucial systems appear to be approaching their tipping points. If one system crashes, it is likely to drag others down, triggering a cascade of chaos known as systemic environmental collapse. This is what happened during previous mass extinctions. [...] Regardless of which complex system is being studied, there's a way of telling whether it is approaching a tipping point. Its outputs begin to flicker. The closer to its critical threshold it comes, the wilder the fluctuation. What we've seen this year is a great global flickering, as Earth systems begin to break down. The heat domes over the western seaboard of North America; the massive fires there, in Siberia and around the Mediterranean; the lethal floods in Germany, Belgium, China, Sierra Leone – these are the signals that, in climatic morse code, spell "mayday".

You might expect an intelligent species to respond to these signals swiftly and conclusively, by radically altering its relationship with the living world. But this is not how we function. Our great intelligence, our highly evolved consciousness that once took us so far, now works against us.

[...] It scarcely matters how green you think you are. The main cause of your environmental impact isn't your attitude. It isn't your mode of consumption. It isn't the choices you make. It's your money. If you have surplus money, you spend it. While you might persuade yourself that you are a green mega-consumer, in reality you are just a mega-consumer. This is why the environmental impacts of the very rich [...] are massively greater than those of everyone else.

Preventing more than 1.5C of global heating means that our average emissions should be no greater than two tonnes of carbon dioxide per person per year. But the richest 1% of the world's people produce an average of more than 70 tonnes. Bill Gates, according to one estimate, emits almost 7,500 tonnes of CO_2, mostly from flying in his private jets. [...] The multiple homes that ultra-rich people own might be fitted with solar panels, their supercars might be electric, their private planes might run on biokerosene, but these tweaks make little difference to the overall impact of their consumption. In some cases, they increase it. The switch to biofuels favoured by Bill Gates is now among the greatest causes of habitat destruction, as forests are felled to produce wood pellets and liquid fuels, and soils are trashed to make biomethane. [...]

The difficult truth is that, to prevent climate and ecological catastrophe, we need to level down. We need to pursue what the Belgian philosopher Ingrid Robeyns calls limitarianism. Just as there is a poverty line below which no one should fall, there is a wealth line above which no one should rise. What we need are not carbon taxes, but wealth taxes. [...] But wealth taxes strike at the heart of the issue. They should be high enough to break the spiral of accumulation and redistribute the riches accumulated by a few. They could be used to put us on an entirely different track, one that I call "private sufficiency, public luxury". While there is not enough ecological or even physical space on Earth for everyone to enjoy private luxury, there is enough to provide everyone with public luxury: magnificent parks, hospitals, swimming pools, art galleries, tennis courts and transport systems, playgrounds and community centres. We should each have our own small domains – private sufficiency – but when we want to spread our wings, we could do so without seizing resources from other people. In consenting to the continued destruction of our life-support systems, we accommodate the desires of the ultra-rich and the powerful corporations they control. [...] We will endure only if we cease to consent. The 19th-century democracy campaigners knew this, the suffragettes knew it, Gandhi knew it, Martin Luther King knew it. The environmental protesters who demand systemic change have also grasped this fundamental truth. In Fridays for Future, Green New Deal Rising, Extinction Rebellion and the other global uprisings against systemic environmental collapse, we see people, mostly young people, refusing to consent. What they understand is history's most important lesson. Our survival depends on disobedience.

(788 words)

Source: *The Guardian*, 30 October 2021

Transcripts

Track 01

Topic 1, Sustainable fashion

1

To be honest, I think the media exaggerates all these negative fast fashion stories. Yeah, my local store sells cheap clothes and I buy them. The only label I look at is the price label. They cost so little because they use low quality materials and I guess they're made in less-developed countries. That's all. I think the media just like to look down on poor people, you know? Fast food – fat, lazy slobs. Fast fashion – people who don't care about sweatshops, et cetera. It's a media invention.

2

Fashion is fashion. If it looks stylish and good on me, I'll buy it. I don't think about fast or slow fashion. Some things are only in for a short time, like one summer maybe, so why would I pay a lot for something I'll only wear once or twice. That's the only time I think about price. Other than that – style is more important.

3

Fast fashion? Not anymore. You see these clothes on me now? They're not even mine – they're pre-loved! I borrowed them through a clothes exchange app – it's really cool and doesn't cost much, especially if you've got nice clothes that you can lend to others. Sharing is caring – caring for the environment, and it's definitely the way of the future. More and more people are joining in.

4

I don't know much about fast fashion, but what I can tell you is the problem is much wider than just cheap clothes. It's our whole throw-away culture that's the issue. One day we want this product right now, the next day it's something different. Clothes, shoes, phones, gadgets. We can't keep buying so much stuff!

5

It doesn't matter what I do – stores sell fast fashion because millions of people buy it. I'm only one person. How am I supposed to know if my clothes were made in a sweatshop, or by kids? I bet the store doesn't even know – or want to know – where their suppliers get the clothes. I just want to live my life. I don't need all this negativity and stress. I don't care anymore.

Track 02

Topic 2, Genetically modified food

Interviewer: The discussion about genetically modified food has become more heated recently. Why do you think that is, Linda?

Linda: Well, the government has loosened some of the restrictions around GMOs and around gene-editing in plants and animals, so that has sparked more debate, and more … exaggerations about the risks, I'm afraid.

Interviewer: So you don't think there are any risks?

Linda: No, that's not what I'm saying. Of course, there are risks. There are always risks when you manipulate DNA. But science in this area is very tightly regulated. And it should be. But, you know, let's look at one example – the GM potato modified to be resistant to the potato-blight disease. That has been through 4,400 risk assessments in 71 countries. Not only that, it has been consumed by more than 350 million people for over 25 years and no increased risk to the environment and no ill-effects on human health have been discovered.

Interviewer: OK, Linda. The potato is safe. So why are people still worried?

Linda: I don't think the problem is the science. The problem is the public's lack of faith in the information they're given. Or the disinformation, maybe I should say.

Interviewer: Disinformation from the government?!

Linda: No, no, no. No, I mean I could tell you now that I, as a scientist, believe the current GMO foods are as safe as organic foods, or the prime minister could say that. But on social media or in tabloid newspapers ordinary people will see these exaggerated scare stories about Frankenstein foods and other public health issues, you know, vaccines or 5G or whatever. It's all nonsense, but it constantly undermines the facts and the solid science. A lot of people just don't know who to believe anymore.

Interviewer: I see what you mean. But you, as a scientist, you don't see any grounds for these fears?

Linda: I understand why people could be worried. That's natural. But the government is right in this case to speed up trials of GM foods, because we just don't have the time to breed drought-resistant and disease-resistant crops the old-fashioned way.

Interviewer:	Why do you say that?
Linda:	Global heating is threatening harvests – there are more droughts, more wildfires. Insects that destroyed crops near the equator are moving north. Crop diseases are getting more common. But during forty years of research, we've developed safe new foods that can withstand drought, that can survive disease. The truth is that food security is no longer only an issue for poor countries in the developing world. We saw that with the Covid-19 pandemic and the Ukraine situation, supermarkets ran out of basic items such as baking products, sunflower oil, pasta. That happened *here* in the UK – a rich, western country. This is an issue for us all and we need to harness the technology we've developed and put it into action faster. Or we'll all face a food crisis.

Track 03

Topic 3, Intercultural competence in the workplace

Exercise 1

People, especially people in the west, think that because you can find a Starbucks and a McDonald's in every city around the world and because we all stream the same blockbusters and TV shows that somehow the world has accepted a common culture: a Western culture. But that's not true. Cultural differences still exist and must be respected. I think my training helps to shake people out of this belief that the western way of doing business has become the norm when it really hasn't.

I learned this the hard way during my business career and have been to every continent on the planet. I've got the professional and personal experience to help people avoid the mistakes I made.

Intercultural training and all this awareness raising is a big moneymaking business. People pay thousands to do weekend courses to qualify as so-called 'experts'. What they're really paying for is a licence to print money. Intercultural competence trainers get paid stacks of money to train businesspeople. But what are they really training people in? It's only common sense in an expensive package. Preparation and planning is normal in *any* business project and visiting a foreign culture is no different. This special training is a waste of money when everything you need to know is on the internet. And don't forget – the people you're visiting, if they're sensible, will have done some research on your culture too. So with a little bit of mutual respect, any small cultural

misunderstandings won't stand in the way of doing business successfully.

Track 04

Exercise 2

Interviewer	I'm talking to two workers here in a multinational corporation who have just finished an intercultural awareness training session. Can you tell me what you thought of it?
Speaker 1	I found it really interesting. I thought I was pretty knowledgeable about other cultures, but the training definitely challenged a lot of my assumptions about myself. It reminded us to be sensitive to differences. You shouldn't trust stereotypes of other cultures, you know. It made us aware of negative bias towards some cultures that we didn't even know we had.
Speaker 2	To be honest, I thought it was a waste of time. The training focused too much on doing business abroad. Our workforce is very diverse, but the training didn't tackle the intercultural issues we have in our teams. Someone complained about a lack of respect for different cultures in our company and the trainer ignored it. The training should focus more on the everyday discrimination that people face here.

Track 05

Topic 4, Gun control in the US

Exercise 1

1   just under two-thirds
2   one in five
3   three point five million
4   a majority
5   81%
6   roughly a quarter
7   39%

Track 06

Exercise 3

The president attended a meeting of his administration's Gun Violence Prevention task force this morning. In his opening remarks, he said gun violence was a national shame and called it an epidemic. He also welcomed the attendance of relatives of some of the one hundred and six people to have died in shooting incidents so far this year, including twenty-six children. While there has been universal condemnation of the deaths, the American public and their politicians in particular remain polarized over the issue of gun law reform.

A recently published survey revealed that three in ten American adults own at least one gun. The survey also showed that ownership of a firearm can be a good indicator of a person's political beliefs. 44% of Republican voters own a gun, but for Democrat supporters the figure is just one in five. Researchers say that 65% of gun owners gave personal protection as the main reason for having a gun, while four in ten said hunting or sport. Only 5% said they needed a gun in relation to their employment.

How do the American people feel about current laws around gun control? Just under half of people surveyed feel that gun violence is a *very* serious problem affecting the United States. A majority – 53% – say that laws around guns need to be stricter. But those views are not evenly spread between Republican and Democratic voters. 81% of Democrats support stricter gun laws. Republicans feel quite differently. Only 20% are in favour of stronger restrictions on firearms. Half say they think the current laws are strong enough and don't need to be changed. A quarter even say gun laws are *too* strict and are in favour of more liberal rules.

Track 07

Topic 5, The British Empire

1

I'm not too pushed about it either way to tell you the truth. History is history and we can't go back and change it. These are things that happened what … a hundred years ago, more – two hundred. It wasn't me or my generation. Haven't we got better things to be worrying about now? I think it's talked about by the people who just want to make issues and arguments out of things. Like, people on one side say we are 'great' Britain and you have to stand up and be proud, fly the flag and what have you – and on the other side they say if you do that you're racist or a white supremacist. Let them all attack each other on social media. It makes no difference to me, I'm too busy to care about it.

2

If you ask me, I'd say that although some terrible things were done to some people in places like India, and the whole slavery trade was absolutely awful. I do think that, you know, the British Empire wasn't all … negative. Plenty of good things were done, and we shouldn't lose sight of those in our rush to criticize the bad things. We built infrastructure, laid the foundations of administration and government, you know? Of course, nobody would think it right to go over to another country now and take it over, but those were different times and people saw things differently then. So, you know, I've got some pride about the positive things and

… like … I feel bad about the things that shouldn't have happened, naturally.

3

We'll never make a better world if we can't look back on the shameful parts of our history and admit that what we did was utterly wrong and abhorrent, frankly. In Germany, they don't shy away from teaching children about the crimes against humanity that the Nazis carried out. It should be the same in British schools. We have to be open about how Britain stole resources from all over the world, how we committed genocide and crimes like slavery. We have to learn from history … to make a better future. And I'd add that, with Britain being multicultural now and all, that we owe it to our fellow Britons – those whose parents came from the old colonies or whose ancestors suffered under the Empire – we owe it to them to respect their history, you know, as part of ours.

4

The British Empire? You mean the English empire? It wasn't the Irish or Scottish or Welsh going over and conquering places, it was the English, mainly. Don't get me wrong, though. I don't mean the ordinary English; I mean the ones at the top. You have to go back to Elizabeth the First, the world as it was then. And they didn't just do it over in India, or Africa or the West Indies first. They started with their neighbours – Ireland, Scotland, Wales. I sound very anti-English, don't I? I'm not really. The issue of colonialism and Empire – it's not just a British thing. There was no European country that behaved acceptably during that era. The whole notion of empire was wrong to begin with, treating countries and people like possessions. So, I guess I'm not proud of the British Empire, but I don't believe anyone in any other country would be proud of what their country did during that period of history.

5

I think focusing on the legacy of the British Empire is misplaced. My grandparents came from the West Indies in the fifties, and I can tell you the consequences of the Empire aren't all in the past. Look at Windrush – there are still people suffering from that. Just look at how the government treats immigrants today – their so-called 'hostile environment'. Right now, they're putting people on planes and flying them to Jamaica even though they were born here in the UK, lived their whole lives here and never set eyes on Jamaica! I know they say that's only people who've been convicted of crimes, but still. It's inhumane. If we really want to address the legacy of the Empire, we need to do something concrete. Proper apologies to the people in the countries we colonized for a start and reparations. Britain is the country it is today because it exploited the resources of those countries, so we should set aside 1% or something of our GDP every year to fund development and infrastructure in those countries we stole from. That would be constructive and actually do some good in return for the harm we caused.

Track 08

Topic 6, Equality

Exercise 1b

racism
diversity
LGBTQ
majority
prejudice
buys
ethnic
inclusivity

Track 09

Exercise 3

Harriet Thanks for joining us today, Anne. You've been reading the latest research on equality in the workplace, and you find the results worrying. Can you tell our listeners why?

Anne Yes, Harriet. I think the main thing which concerns me is that there's a perception out there that we are making more progress towards an equal society than we actually are.

Harriet OK, but which results exactly in the research make you say that?

Anne There's a report just published by the British Management Institute, and one third of employees surveyed said they had been victims of bias or negative treatment due to their identity. That's equivalent to 6.9 million British workers.

Harriet What effects did this treatment have?

Anne It had different effects on those looking for work and those in work. Large majorities of British Black or Asian workers feel they are passed over for employment opportunities, and if they are in jobs, they don't get promoted. Members of the LGBTQ plus community report greater levels of harassment and bullying. The report went into details on some of the issues. To name just two examples, some Black interviewees cite their hairstyles and some Asian workers the fact they don't drink alcohol as key factors.

Harriet Not drinking? I would've thought that would be seen as positive by an employer.

Anne Not if it means the worker misses out on networking opportunities – who do you think is more likely to get a promotion: the non-drinking Muslim colleague or the colleague who goes for the Friday afternoon pint after work to the pub with the manager?

Harriet I see what you mean. And people with natural black hairstyles are experiencing discrimination?

Anne Indeed. Many black workers said employers viewed hairstyles such as dreads, Afros or cornrows as unprofessional. Some called for the British government to include hair discrimination in anti-discrimination legislation – just as some states in the US have already done.

Harriet Before our interview started, Anne, you mentioned there'd been a new study on the gender pay gap?

Anne Yes, Harriet, that's right. While there is evidence to say the gender pay gap is narrowing – women earned 6.5% less than men in 2011 but 4.6% two years ago – this general progress is not reflected in the situation of women from ethnic minorities. I'm afraid to say the opposite is the case. The Economics Institute says that British women with a Pakistani or Bangladeshi background are paid less than their white British counterparts and the gap is actually bigger now than 25 years ago.

Harriet That's pretty depre-

Anne And workers with a disability ... sorry Anne, I interrupted you.

Harriet It's OK. I was just going to say that it's pretty depressing.

Anne I'll come back to you on that. But first, I didn't want to leave out people with disabilities. 34% of disabled people in the Management Institute's survey said they also experience hostile or derogatory attitudes from colleagues.

Harriet Are we making any progress at all, Anne?

Anne In their conclusions, the Institute say that, apart from the racial element in the gender pay gap, most indicators show that the situation in general trends towards more equality. Certainly, recent changes to the law mean inclusion and equality are no longer ... optional but required. So it's not all depressing. I think, in a way the tools are there to help Britain become a truly equal society... em ...

Harriet I feel a 'but' coming ...

Anne   Yeah, the law has finally caught up, but if we really want to get to that equal society, we – you and me and our listeners – we need to tackle everyday racism and discrimination, you know? Challenge negative attitudes towards minority groups that our family members, neighbours and colleagues might have – even if – and maybe especially if they are not aware of it. I also support the Management Institute's call for businesses to take more proactive steps to increase the number of women, LGBTQ plus and ethnic minorities in senior management and on executive boards.

Harriet   Yes. Well, I'm a bit relieved that things are going in the right direction, even if they are moving more slowly than we'd like. And what you said about everyday discrimination – I think we should all bear that in mind. Thanks again for coming into the studio, Anne, and coming up next we'll have a little music from a young band from Newcastle called …
[FADE OUT]

Track 10

Mock exam

Task 1 - GM food

Speaker 1   GM food has been around for twenty years and the Frankenstein plants that all the doomsayers predicted haven't appeared. We took vaccines against Covid – some of those were genetically engineered. We didn't drop dead, did we? Trust science and calm down on the fear, man.

Speaker 2   I know there are problems making sure everybody on the planet has enough to eat. But we don't need GM to help grow more food. We already have enough – the problem is distributing the food to the people who need it. We in the West have more than enough. We just waste a lot of it through our selfishness.

Speaker 3   Genetically modified food is an absolute disgrace. Why would you change something that's natural? It's dangerous messing around in laboratories, creating these … these artificial plants. And animals too even! It's Pandora's box, isn't it? Once something really bad escapes – that's it. We could destroy ourselves.

Speaker 4   I don't have a problem with genetically engineered food, to be honest. But I do have an issue with big corporations having the patents on these new foods. You know what I mean? It's just another money-making scheme. A big corporation convinces small farmers to plant only their brand of GM crop, but then the farmer discovers that every year he has to buy more seed from the company. Those corporations are like drug dealers.

Speaker 5   I'm not worried about GMOs, no more than I am about climate change. We've changed our planet so much as it is that it's a little too late to start worrying now. We've put so many chemicals and pesticides into our air and soil, for example. What difference will GM make? Not much. You would have to move to Antarctica or the deepest Amazon to have a pure, natural environment.

Track 11

Task 2 - The UK and the Windrush Generation

I was only nine years old when my mum gathered me and my brothers around her to give us some important advice. She looked at us one by one, looked in our eyes, pointed at us and said: "You have to integrate, boys. You must mix with the people of Portsmouth. Talk *to* them, talk *like* them, eat what *they* eat and do what *they* do. But whatever you do, don't be different."

It was the sixties, and I did what I was told. I integrated, I changed my voice, I dressed like other kids and I didn't do anything to stand out … well, stand out any more than being one of the few Black faces in the town. But integrating came with a price tag. As I was becoming more and more British, I was losing more and more of what made me Jamaican.

My mother moved from her home and when she did, she gave up much more than the sun and the sea to build a new life here in cold, wet England for her family. Like so many Caribbean people then and after, who faced constant racism and adversity, she wasn't going to back down or walk away from our shot at happiness. But she never took the advice she gave us, she always remained a proud Jamaican, through and through.

During those hard times, my mum and dad never gave us kids any sign that anything was ever wrong. It was only later that I understood when Mum and Dad needed to talk privately about "Big People's Business", they were protecting us from the realities they had to face.

As part of my television work, I wanted to understand why my parents wanted us to integrate so much, so I did a lot of research. Watching hours of old TV news stories and reading hundreds of newspapers from those days, it became clearer to me. Integration is so much easier than constantly having to fight. The Windrush generation pushed us so hard so that my brothers and I and all the other Black kids wouldn't have to.

As a kid, I remember how the British and the Jamaican worlds, so to speak, seemed apart – separate and I remember how that seemed to change – slowly. When I was around thirteen, there used to be only one Black Caribbean performer who you would often see on British TV. He used to appear regularly on an entertainment show and sing funny songs about life in Britain in calypso style, a traditional Jamaican type of music. A few years later, a white English comedy performer started using a fake Jamaican accent to sing calypso songs about the news in a weekly TV programme. Of course, that wouldn't be allowed now because it's cultural appropriation, but it showed me that Jamaican culture was slowly but surely influencing mainstream British society.

When I began my own career in entertainment fifty years ago, my audiences were mainly white. My first comedy routines were usually impressions and jokes about myself and other Black people. I even remember telling an audience: "You'd better laugh, or I'll move into the house beside you – then you'll get a lower price when you try to sell!" Without realizing it, I was taking the everyday racism we had to live with and turning it into comedy for white people. I can see that now, but I didn't see it then.

I'm embarrassed to say it was only when I really hit the big time and performed in front of the royal family that a hero of mine – the late Arnold Williams – came to me after the show and told me: "You're really great, but you don't have to tell those jokes for anyone. Just be yourself."

That made me realize that if I was going to build a career in the British mainstream, my best chance was to be true to myself. That instead of making jokes to make white people laugh at me, I should celebrate my Black Britishness. Since then, I've tried to make my comedy more inclusive and make us Britons laugh with each other more. It's a journey that all of us are on, together.

Track 12

Task 3 - The gig economy

Tom Hi, I'm Tom. I'm forty-five and I became a 'gig worker' around ten years ago.

Interviewer Ten years? And before that?

Tom Well, I graduated at 22 with a degree in architecture, I joined a construction firm and, you know, for the first decade or so of my career I sort of fell for the traditional American Dream-stuff they teach you to believe.

Interviewer Which is?

Tom You know – you work like a hamster on a wheel for forty years and … and your reward is your retirement. Like, you can discover the world when you're old and grey. Lucky for me the financial crisis came along in oh-eight and oh-nine.

Interviewer Why 'lucky you'? They were hard times for a lot of folks.

Tom Yeah, I suppose it's weird to say that it was lucky for me, but it turned out that way. You see I was let go from my job in the recession of 2009. Escaping that cushy, routine nine-to-five job was the best thing that ever happened me. It forced me to think outside the box and come up with other options. I've been working gigs ever since.

Interviewer You make it sound very positive. Was it easy?

Tom (laughs) Easy? Man, no way was it easy. I had so little money – I even went hungry at first. But I couldn't face the thought of going through interview after interview, looking for a new cage to be trapped in, you know? I did a lot of reflecting. From that I realized that it was my passion for art and drawing that first got me into architecture. So I reconnected with that passion inside me and started drawing again. I had always been a geek on Facebook and Yelp, so I simply learned how to exploit them as a business owner rather than a consumer. You gotta remember this was before influencers and social media stars took everything over. So I promoted my artwork online, started selling pieces, then I realized people wanted to learn, so I organized workshops. It even expanded to become a school of sorts.

Interviewer But you don't run a school now, do you? I thought …

Tom (laughs again) No, no. I was kinda a victim of my own success. That became too much of a headache, too busy, no freedom, so I jacked that in. But the whole project had opened my eyes to the possibilities. It got me involved in the cultural sphere. Now I manage a professional website focused on cultural events and programs for communities of color and immigrants. It's sort of underneath the mainstream radar if you know what I mean. That work led to another gig I do – working as a diversity consultant in the arts.

Interviewer I was going to say I thought you hadn't left architecture behind completely.

Tom I haven't. That's another hat I wear. I'm a field technician for an architectural company. That pays most of my bills actually, but it's not like my other gigs – less passion.

Interviewer But you're not actually an employee, are you?

Tom	That's correct. I'm an external contractor with a rolling short-term contract. I'd hate to have to rely only on that – that's no way to live. But, for me with my other work, it works out. That's the nature of the beast: *gigging* means that you have to accept some work that you don't necessarily love but that is going to help keep you afloat so that you can dedicate yourself to work you prefer.
Interviewer	So ... although you've been quite positive, life's tough as a gig worker?
Tom	Obviously, it's not everyone's cup of tea but no one ever said life was easy, did they? Sure, I don't get sick leave and I don't often make myself take time out. Yeah, and working multiple jobs, I'm probably not as healthy as I should be. (*laughs*) But at the end of the day, I'm my own boss and I'm no one's hamster.

Bildquellen

Lines for writing tasks

Verfasser	Peadar Curran
Beraterin	Alexandra Köpf, Seminar für Ausbildung und Fortbildung der Lehrkräfte Weingarten; Friedrich-List Schule, Ulm
Redaktion	Daniel Shatwell
Redaktionelle Mitarbeit	Christine House
Projektleitung	Andreas Goebel
Umschlaggestaltung	Rosendahl, Berlin
Coverfoto	Shutterstock/Lewis Liu
Layout	Klein & Halm Grafikdesign, Berlin
Technische Umsetzung	Straive, Chennai

Andere Begleitmaterialien für Schülerinnen und Schüler zu Crossover Band 2:

E-Book des Schülerbuchs   ISBN 978-3-06-452111-7

www.cornelsen.de

1. Auflage, 1. Druck 2022

Alle Drucke dieser Auflage sind inhaltlich unverändert und können im Unterricht nebeneinander verwendet werden.

© 2022 Cornelsen Verlag GmbH, Berlin

Druck: Athesiadruck GmbH

ISBN 978-3-06-452113-1

PEFC zertifiziert
Dieses Produkt stammt aus nachhaltig bewirtschafteten Wäldern und kontrollierten Quellen.

PEFC
PEFC/18-31-166

www.pefc.de

1 crossover 6th edition

ANSWER KEY

Topic 1

Getting to grips with grammar

1

1 Non-renewable energy sources are those <u>derived</u> from fossil fuels such as oil, coal and natural gas.
2 <u>Taking</u> millions of years to form, they are limited in quantity and at some point will run out.
3 Mining these fuels causes terrible damage to the environment, <u>disturbing</u> ecosystems and <u>harming</u> wildlife.
4 When <u>burned</u>, fossil fuels produce large amounts of pollution <u>known</u> as greenhouse gases, because they trap heat in the atmosphere.
5 <u>Alarmed</u> by climate change, environmentalists say the use of fossil fuels has to stop *now*.
6 <u>Coming</u> from natural elements such as the sun, the wind or water, renewable energy will never run out and it is clean, <u>producing</u> no harmful emissions.
7 Nuclear energy does not create polluting gases, but the radioactive waste <u>left</u> behind will stay dangerous for thousands of years, <u>meaning</u> future generations will have to deal with it.

2

breaking – being – answering – to look – to start – to open – missing

3 a

1 Bats first passed Ebola on to humans in the 1970s.
2 People in West Africa were slaughtering gorillas and chimpanzees for food.
3 The Covid-19 pandemic has wiped trillions of dollars from the global economy.
4 Lassa fever infects between 300,000 and 500,000 people in West Africa every year.
5 Scientists and economists have estimated the cost of preventing future pandemics over the next ten years to be 2% of the financial damage caused by Covid-19.

3 b

1 i) It is believed that the Amazon rainforest produces 25% of …
   ii) The Amazon rainforest is believed to produce 25% of …
2 i) It is thought that the Amazon region is home …
   ii) The Amazon region is thought to be home …
3 i) It is estimated that the Amazon rainforest loses tens of millions …
   ii) The Amazon rainforest is estimated to lose tens of millions …

4 i) It has been claimed that a third of all emerging diseases are the result …
   ii) A third of all emerging diseases have been claimed to be the result …
5 i) It wasn't expected that the Covid-19 pandemic would last longer than a year.
   ii) The Covid-19 pandemic wasn't expected to last longer than a year.
6 i) It has been said that Covid-19 and HIV share their origins …
   ii) Covid-19 and HIV have been said to share their origins …

Dealing with visual material

1

A silhouette	E outline
B out of focus	F vibrant
C expressive	G juxtaposition
D shaped like sth	H superimposed over

2 a

photo – quotation – centre – shaped – resemble – on – appears – surrounding – looks – At – says – quotation

2 b

1. altered – 2. caused – 3. conveys – 4. help – 5. reinforces – 6. evoke

2 c

In my opinion, the image is effective in conveying its message because of the combination of the striking image and the quotation. The juxtaposition of the healthy green trees with the 'sick' barren landscape is particularly successful in emphasizing how much we rely on forests for our survival. The element of brown 'sickness' infecting the 'lung' on the right works very well because it echoes the warning in President Roosevelt's quotation – we are in danger of destroying ourselves if we do not stop deforestation.

Writing workshop 1

2

Rhetorical devices:	**A** use of pronouns
	B contrast/antithesis
	G rhetorical questions
Structural devices:	**H** parallelism
	I concluding call to action/appeal
	C repetition/anaphora
Imagery:	**D** metaphors, **F** symbolism
Sound devices:	**E** alliteration

3

1. antithesis
2. anaphora
3. metaphors
4. symbolism
5. rhetorical question
6. parallelism
7. climax

4

freie Lösung

Writing workshop 2

1

The letter writer is annoyed and thinks that the magazine article was a waste of time for several reasons: knowing a geological term does not do anything to help us be greener, and climate sceptics do not believe in science so this name change will not make them change their behaviour. The writer wants the magazine to focus more on practical actions that people can take to protect the environment.

2

a. **Combining supporting arguments**
   darüber hinaus: furthermore
   nicht nur …, sondern auch: not only … but also
   ähnlich: similarly
   überdies/ferner: moreover
   zusätzlich (zu): in addition (to)

b. **Contrasting opposing arguments**
   im Gegensatz dazu: on the contrary
   nichtsdestotrotz: nevertheless
   während/wogegen/indessen: whereas
   trotz der Tatsache, dass: despite the fact that
   einerseits … anderseits: on the one hand … on the other hand

3 a

people who are sceptical …: con
the Anthropocene …: pro
If you changed the name …: con
some newspapers …: pro
nobody cares …: con
we need to educate …: pro

3 b

On the one hand, supporters say the Anthropocene name is based on hard facts and we should use every piece of evidence to convince people to care about our planet. On the other hand, people who are sceptical of man-made climate change won't care about changing one scientific name.

Supporters say on the contrary, some newspapers use the words 'heating' and 'crisis' instead of 'warming' and 'change'. Words have power and this power can influence not only people's opinions but also

government policies. Nevertheless, it could be argued that nobody cares about these strange names; they worry about today's and tomorrow's problems instead.

Despite the fact that Anthropocene is just a word, renaming our epoch can be part of a learning process; we need to educate people about how we are affecting the planet and declaring a new epoch could be part of that education.

In conclusion, having looked at both sides of the argument, my own view is that although words do have power, this one word will not make a constructive difference. Rather than making changes to what we call our era, I think we should focus on making changes to how we live.

Dealing with listening tasks

2

b, d, e

3

child labour, sustainable, throw-away culture, the third world, suppliers, sweatshops, lend/borrow clothes, charity shops

4

1E, 2F, 3B, 4D, 5A

Words in context

2

blame
belief: to (dis-)believe (vb); believer (n); (dis-)believing (adj); (un-)believable (adj)
environment: environmental (adj), environmentally (adv)
eco-
emission: to emit (vb)
greenhouse: Carbon dioxide is called a greenhouse gas because …

3

1d, 2a, 3e, 4c, 5b

The chill out zone

1

1A, 2C, 3B, 4E, 5D

2

2. disposable
3. overconsumption
4. pre-loved
5. recyclable
6. renewable
7. unethical
8. untreated

Getting to grips with grammar

1

2 Having received approval from the US FDA, the first consumer GMO, a genetically engineered human insulin to treat diabetes, went on sale in 1982.

3 Having begun with GM tomatoes in 1994, the sale of GMO foods became more widespread in the US in the 1990s.

4 Having been used in a variety of crops, genetic engineering was first approved in an animal, salmon, for human consumption in 2015.

5 Having accumulated over 25 years of experience in GMO foods, the FDA began considering the next step in GMO science – editing the genes of organisms themselves – in 2019.

6 Having only allowed one GM corn crop for many years, the EU has gradually expanded the range of GMOs cultivated and sold in its member states.

2

2 Lori said that there to talk with her that day was the Head of PR of Vegan World.

3 Lori asked Simon / Lori wanted to know what steps Simon/he was taking to make eating vegetarian more appealing.

4 Simon said / Simon told Lori that they had found that a big part of the problem then was how plant-based meat was marketed.

5 Lori asked him/Simon / Lori wanted to know what he meant.

6 Simon said / Simon told Lori that up until then, most marketing had presented the product as "meat-free", but they had found that to be very ineffective.

7 Simon said / Simon told Lori / explained that it/that made people focus on what they were not getting and that it was important that the consumers could focus on what they were getting.

8 Lori asked Simon to give / if he could give her an example of that.

9 Simon said / Simon told Lori that they had decided to try out a few different names and it had made a huge difference.

3

2 (non-defining) Dogs, which were … forty thousand years ago, will never …

3 (defining) … robot dogs that were programmed to make sure people socially distance frightened children …

4 (non-defining) … robot artist Ai-Da, which was named after the mathematician Ada Lovelace, hosted its own …

5 (non-defining) Last year, however, Ai-Da, which uses cameras for eyes, was stopped …

6 (defining) A Wittenberg church introduced a robot that beamed lights from its hand to give blessings to people to mark the 500th anniversary …

7 (defining) … racist and sexist comments that it had learned from humans.

8 (non-defining) … the incident, which happened in 2016, was a valuable learning experience …

Mediating a text: From German to English

1

etw recherchieren: to research sth
aktuell: current
etw bekommen: to receive sth
eventuell: possibly
etw organisieren: to organize sth
sensibel: sensitive
also: so

2

b Gründe anführen, warum man etwas nicht befürwortet; etwas kritisieren

c to refuse to see a problem or refuse to deal with it

d to give an opinion about something / everything, even if other people do not want to hear it

3

Audience: fellow students and foreign students
Text type: summary of one German author's opinion
Aim: to provide advice/arguments
Register: more formal
Content: risks of smart home relevant to data privacy and security

4

Security: Smart security systems which turn lights on and off automatically can be noticed by criminals and act like a sign saying, "Please rob this house!". People do not take enough care with their wireless security, and they often click too quickly on service agreements, without reading them.

Privacy: In the US some front door cameras send their videos to police stations – it is important to know what happens to your data. We must keep in mind that the manufacturers of smart systems could try to make money from our data, even if it is anonymous. Companies can analyse people's online habits and can manipulate us into buying things. When we share our data, it is at risk if the companies which have it are hacked.

Writing workshop 1

1

The author's aim and the purpose of the text is both to inform and persuade the reader. The author informs readers that her company is "one of the many companies offering alternatives to meat" (ll. 2–3) but she goes on to say that is "not all" (l. 3) that it is. She seeks to persuade readers that her company offers a vision and a strategy "to reverse humanity's dangerous course" (l. 4) away from "climate disaster" (l. 5). Towards the end of her text, she demonstrates that she wants to persuade readers because she asks both supporters and sceptics to "keep communicating" (l. 38) and offers a link for more information.

2

The author employs an informal register. This is illustrated by her opening her 'letter' with "Dear Friends … Strangers", her use of contracted forms (we'd – we would, would've – would have, etc.) and informal and slang words (kidding, folks, cow farts). I think she uses it to establish a close relationship with her readers so that they will be more open to listening to her arguments and agreeing with her.

3

a – 4 – v	d – 3 – ii
b – 5 – iv	e – 1 – iii
c – 2 – i	

4

1	engages	7	descriptive
2	poses	8	explains
3	solutions	9	conclusion
4	orders	10	problem
5	cause and effect	11	appeals
6	present		

5

1	sentimental	5	warning
2	optimistic	6	witty
3	humorous	7	urgent
4	serious		

6

Answers should refer to some/all of the following:
Language (stylistic devices employed): <u>direct address of the reader</u> ("If you don't know us …"); <u>alliteration</u> ("combined climate cost", "wild, wonderful green", "growth of green plants", "give humanity a helping hand", "supporter or sceptic"); <u>contrast</u> (all the positives and none of the negatives"); <u>enumeration</u> ("through extinctions, intensive farming and overfishing"); <u>exaggeration</u> ("we would set off an explosion of wild, wonderful green"); <u>imagery</u> ("this beautiful blue, white and green ship", "explosion of wild, wonderful green"); <u>metaphor</u> ("this beautiful … ship", "away from the brink", "pathways", "doomsday clock", "clicking our fingers", "the asteroid", "helping hand"); <u>parallelism</u> ("that's what we are, but that's not all we are"); rhetorical question ("Who can argue with a win-win proposition like that?")

Structure: Exercise 4 provides an example of analysing how structure can be employed by an author in a persuasive text.

Writing workshop 2

1

informal vocabulary and style, introduction – body – conclusion, written to be read by a large audience, personal tone, contains your personal opinion on a topic, contracted grammatical forms

2

provided that: as long as
however: but
nevertheless: anyway
consequently: so
in addition to that: as well as that
moreover: on top of that
in conclusion: all in all
therefore: that's why

3

perspective: from my own perspective
purpose: to give my own opinion on whether robots can be our friends
audience: my fellow students, our families and the teachers

5

Introduction/Opening: Consider what the question means to me – could a robot replace my best friends?! Joke
Connector: I've got friends, but others might not have.
Main body: Paragraph 1 → useful ways robots could be companions for lonely or sick people
Paragraph 2 → Robots shouldn't replace real relationships / not be too human / privacy rules
Conclusion: My opinion in one sentence. Funny closing.

6

When I think about this question, I can't help but think to myself which of my human best friends could a robot ever replace? Bobby, if you're reading this, don't worry! Jenny, you know that you still haven't given me back my T-shirt?! Just kidding, everybody. If you're lucky like me, you'll have good friends such as Bobby and Jenny who you'd never replace with a robot. But not everyone is so lucky.

Having social contact isn't so easy for some people, such as the elderly, the ill or people with disabilities. That's why I don't think we should be too quick to say robots could never be our friends. Technology like video calling can help us feel less isolated or alone – think back to the pandemic – and for people who feel lonely, why can't technology in the form of companion robots help them? Many people feel less alone if they have a pet, and pets can't even communicate very much or at all. A robot who could interact and 'speak', even if it wasn't fully intelligent, could give isolated people a sense of companionship and could act as a safety monitor – calling an ambulance if the person had an accident or didn't wake up in the morning.

Before you think I'm completely in favour of robot 'friends', I'd better say that I think we need to be careful. AI ethicists such as Kate Darling say that we shouldn't expect robots to solve social problems such as loneliness or lack of care workers, and I agree with her. Robots should never replace real, human social contact. I don't think robots should have human names as some digital assistants have today, and I also don't believe they should be made to look human – it should always be clear that they are pieces of tech. We've got to keep in mind that businesses will sell these devices for profit, so strict rules should be in place to say what robots are and aren't allowed to do and what personal information they can and can't share.

All in all, I think robots can be useful as companions as long as they don't replace real relationships and there are good rules around them. But Jenny, I still want my T-shirt back or else I might spend your birthday with my new best friend, Technotron!

Dealing with listening tasks

1

Examples: genetically altered, genetic engineering, DNA, biotech/biotechnology, herbicide, pesticides, cross-breeding, patents, risks, benefits, environment, agriculture, pollution, contamination, etc.

2

controversial: problematic, divisive, hot topic, etc.
dangers: risks, threats, harms, etc.
rules: regulations, orders, guidelines, limits, etc.
25 years: a quarter (of a) century, two and a half decades, over two decades, etc.
sensationalist: over the top, exaggerated, (melo) dramatic, blown out of proportion, hyperbolic, etc.
to accelerate: to go faster / at a faster rate, to speed up, to hurry up, to boost, etc.
to breed: to grow, to nurture, to raise, to produce, etc.
drought: dry periods, lack/shortage of rain/water, etc.

3

1 the government has relaxed the rules around it.
2 a GM food that is proven to be safe.
3 destroy people's trust in science with sensationalist stories.
4 breeding new crops in the traditional way is too slow.

5 food security is definitely an urgent issue for everyone everywhere.

Words in context

2

break sth down into sth: break it down into smaller steps
digital: digitize / digitalize (vb), digitization / digitalization (n), digitized (adj), digital (adj), digitally (adv)
imagine: imagination (n), imaginary (adj), (un-) imaginative (adj), (un-)imaginable (adj), unimaginably (adv)
to infringe / privacy / provider

3

recognition, digital, erode, emotion, genuine, audio

4

1 data
2 genuine
3 fooled
4 algorithms
5 facial recognition

The chill out zone

1

a spam
b googol
c nerd
d hacker
e bug
f computer

2

Betrüger: fraudster
Film-/Bildmaterial: footage
Gerät, technischer Krimskrams: gadget
Haushaltsgerät: appliance
Überwachung: surveillance
Widerstand: resistance

Topic 3

Getting to grips with grammar

1

1 In most countries, social media posts which/that advertise brands and products must be labelled with #Ad or #Paid.
2 However, influencers can share their opinions about products and brands (which) they actually use without these hashtags.
3 This raises the question: how can we tell if a post is a genuine product review, which does not need the Ad# label, or a paid-for advertisement?
4 Last September, the UK Advertising Standards Agency checked 122 Instagram influencer accounts and all their posts which were uploaded over a three-week period.

5 The check, which involved looking at 24,000 posts, revealed that only 35% of paid-for advertising posts were correctly labelled as adverts.

6 The agency did not name the people who broke the rules but is thinking about naming-and-shaming them in the future.

2

2 The manager told the employees to use the mute button during online meetings when they weren't/ aren't speaking.

3 The colleague told the woman to report their boss because he was discriminating against her.

4 The workers wanted to know if the company could provide more childcare places for their children.

5 The business expert told the audience not to expect quality to be achieved overnight.

6 The journalist asked how long it would be until all workers had the right to flexible working.

7 The father told his child not to disturb him because he was working.

3

1 well – different	4 wrong – fairly
2 hard – lazy	5 expensive –
3 low – completely	successfully

Dealing with visual material

1

1b, 2d, 3c, 4f, 5e

2

correct: 4, 5; incorrect: 1, 2, 3

3

1 agreement		6	agreement
2 disagreement		7	disagreement
3 agreement		8	clarification
4 clarification		9	clarification
5 disagreement		10	agreement

4

1 I'm not sure the evidence supports your conclusion. The graph shows that 38% of consumers say sustainable fashion is too expensive, but that doesn't mean they don't have the money to buy it. Some of them might have the money but feel the price is too high.

2 I'm afraid I must contradict you because I don't believe the author means we shouldn't care about ethical consumption. The author encourages people to try to be as sustainable as possible but that in a capitalist society we should be realistic.

3 That's an excellent point. / I agree 100% and I would add … / Those are my thoughts too and I would also say … that we should put pressure on large corporations to be more ethical and sustainable as well.

4 That's an excellent point. / When you say 'stuff' what do you mean exactly?

Writing workshop 1

1

1 directly addressing the reader
2 informal register
3 engaging opening
4 expert opinion
5 strong, determined language

2

Technique / Stylistic device: engaging opening
The author begins his / her article by placing the reader in the position of a guest in a funny anecdote (ll. 1–8). This immediately arouses the reader's interest in a very effective way because they will naturally want to know how the short 'story' goes on and ends. It also makes the reader focus on the topic of the text successfully because if they don't drink the horse milk offered to the guests, "it could cost you" (l. 8) the important business deal. Most readers will carry on reading to find out how to handle such situations.

Technique / Stylistic device: expert opinion

The author supports his/her thesis by quoting three successful businessmen and including details of their real-life experience doing business in foreign countries. This makes him/her more credible and makes what is said more convincing. The embarrassing situations the businessmen describe also warn the readers that they should prepare well before doing business abroad, but in a humorous way.

Technique / Stylistic device: directly addressing the reader (ideas only)

makes reader feel involved and affected, increases interest and motivation to read and finish the text, increases impact of message

Technique / Stylistic device: strong, determined language (ideas only)

conveys seriousness and importance of topic, increases reader's interest and makes arguments more forceful and convincing

3

A3, B4, C2, D6

4

Structural device: The author uses a 'problem and solution' structure, presenting the gender pay gap as a problem which employers should recognize, the benefits for their businesses of solving the problem and then offering a possible way of dealing with it.

Expert opinion (Practical argument / statistical information): Although the author doesn't name experts, she does give statistics to show how effective her solution is in closing the pay gap and also how men and women view businesses who do not ask about salary history more positively.

Strong, determined language: The author uses strong language to convey the importance and urgency of the issue: "pernicious", "right now", "compelling", "need to stop", "it absolutely is".

The author uses vocabulary with negative connotations e.g. "pernicious", "damaging", "missing out", "uncomfortable", "unfair" and "damaged" when describing the problem of the gender pay gap. When describing the benefits of solving the pay gap and taking her advice, she uses positively connoted words, e.g. "improves performance and productivity", "effective", "easy", "compelling", "helped", "boost", "benefit", "fairer", "gender equality" and "win-win".

Engaging opening: The author begins with a surprising statistic ("Progress to close … we won't see it done until 2050.") that immediately raises the readers' interest and motivates them to read the full text.

Direct address: The author does not directly address employers but rather employees through the use of the possessive pronoun 'our': "Our answers are most often used". This point would not answer the task because the task refers to convincing employers.

Writing workshop 2

1

Introduction
a My topic today is …
b First, I will address … and then … followed by …
c I would like to speak to you about …

Main part
d First, we need to ask ourselves …
e Now I will turn to …
f We must also take into account that …
g The next point I would like to look at is …

Closing
h Let me close by asking you all a question …
i In conclusion …
j When you consider the arguments I have made, I am sure you will agree that …

2

1	an assumption	6	a certainty
2	a certainty	7	a doubt
3	a doubt	8	an assumption
4	an assumption	9	a certainty
5	a certainty	10	a doubt

3 a

1h, 2c, 3d, 4g, 5b, 6a

3 b

It is a real pleasure to take part in this conference on youth unemployment. <u>My topic today</u> is why we should consider adopting a universal basic income.

<u>First, I will address</u> how such a scheme would work, then I will present the main criticisms followed by the reasons why I think these criticisms are not justified.

<u>First, we need to ask ourselves</u> what the word universal in universal basic income means. Universal means every adult citizen, with no exceptions. Every citizen in our country would receive a basic income. Every adult? Even the rich people who don't need it? I assume you're thinking. The answer is 'yes'. It's not as unusual as you might think. In Germany, the state already pays money known as *Kindergeld* to every family with children, regardless of income or social status. The UBI would be paid with no strings attached – no bureaucracy, no official deciding whether you deserve it, no one putting pressure on you to go out and look for a job. It sounds simple because it is simple.

<u>Now I will turn to</u> some of the arguments put forward by opponents of a UBI. The first argument they would probably make is that it would discourage unemployed people from searching for a job. After all, why should they look for a job when they get money for nothing? <u>They could say there is not much evidence that</u> a UBI would solve unemployment. A trial carried out in Finland showed only a slight increase in the number of people who found jobs while receiving the UBI compared to people who received the normal unemployment benefit. That's true, but it was a small trial and short.

They would also <u>undoubtedly</u> add that it will be too expensive. If it is universal, wealthy people and people with well-paid jobs will receive money they don't need. That won't fix unfairness in society, they could say. They would say that it's a big waste of money which could be spent on poor people and the homeless or on our hospitals and schools.

But, ladies and gentlemen, <u>we must also take into account that</u> the social security system we have today hasn't really solved the problem of fairness, has it? To the opponents of a UBI, I say that it is time to try something new. To them I say that the trial in Finland showed an increase in people successfully finding a job. I admit it was a small increase, but the UBI did not make people sit at home and watch TV like its opponents claimed it would. So after two years, it had a small but positive effect.

Let me turn now to their second criticism – how expensive it would be. <u>It goes without saying that</u> a UBI would be expensive, but we also have to consider how much money we would save. The trial in Finland showed people receiving UBI had a much higher level of well-being. They felt less stress and less insecure. <u>The fact is that</u> people on UBI felt happier and they were healthier. And that means fewer people turning to alcohol and drugs, less crime caused by alcohol and drugs. It means fewer people with mental health problems from anxiety and stress. People wouldn't feel the pressure to take the first job they find – they could instead look longer until they find a job that makes them happy. That all saves our country money and even saves lives.

As I said before, the system is simple. So we wouldn't have to spend so much money on all the current bureaucracy needed to manage the complicated social security system we have today. Workers in our social security system would not have to spend hours and hours making decisions as to who should get unemployment benefit and checking if people are really looking for jobs. Those workers could do other much more useful tasks.

In conclusion, ladies and gentlemen, I think the possible benefits of a UBI outweigh the possible risks. The savings we could make will balance the costs of such a scheme. Our country and other countries have tried the current social system for long enough and unemployment still exists. In our country, every person is equal and deserves to be able to live a good life. <u>When you consider the arguments I have made, I am sure you will agree that</u> the time for a change has come and we should adopt a universal basic income. Thank you.

Dealing with listening tasks

1

- a Cultural differences still exist and must be respected.
  The trainer has the personal experience to help businesses.
- b The training is only common sense.
  It is a waste of money because all the information is available on the internet.

2

- a It reminded people to be sensitive.
  It warned/advised people not to trust cultural stereotypes.
- b It didn't deal with intercultural problems in the company.
  The training should focus more on discrimination.

Words in context

2

brand
consumerism: to consume (vb), consumerism (n), consumer (n), consumption (n)

demand: When demand is greater than supply, the price goes up.
ethical
incentive: incentives
organic

3

surge, concern, chief executive, equivalent, energy-efficient, vegetarian

4

1 stokes demand	4 do business
2 suffered losses	5 growth … bolstered
3 reflect … concerns	

The chill out zone

1

True: 1, 2, 4; False: 3

2

1c, 2e, 3g, 4a, 5b, 6d, 7f

3

a E, b Q, c U, d A, e L, f P, g A, h Y
Equal pay

Topic 4

Getting to grips with grammar

1

The name: If you ask US citizens, many don't know that America …
The flag: His teacher gave him a B minus grade but told him he would raise the grade if the flag was/were accepted as the United States' …
Geography: The US would look very different today if it hadn't bought land: Florida …
The people: The US is seen, rightly or wrongly, as a white country but if current population trends continue, the majority of US citizens will be non-white in twenty-five years'.
Ethnicity: As a group, they would be half the size of Germany's population if you added them together: 43 million.
Traditions: If there hadn't been so much immigration from Germany throughout its history, the US wouldn't have some of its most loved traditions today …

2

1 have never been able to	5 believed
2 received	6 has grown
3 said	7 has just published
4 has fallen	8 described

3

1 Some people – many wars – any peace
2 some hope – any evidence – an improvement
3 some / a lot of progress – a lot of / some work – the damage

Dealing with visual material

1

The quotation is taken from President Joe Biden's inaugural address which he gave on January 20th, 2021. President Biden is urging the American people to listen and respect one another even though they have disagreements.

2

Description: The bar chart shows the percentage of Republicans and Democrats who have had a very negative view of the opposing party over a number of years, beginning in 1994, with the most recent data from 2020. The chart is based on two sources of data, namely, Statista and the Survey Center on American Life. The horizontal axis shows the years 1994, 2004, 2014, 2017 and 2020. The vertical bars are divided into red and blue, red representing Republicans and blue, the Democrats. In 1994, 17% of Republicans viewed the Democratic party very negatively. Ten years later, this had risen slightly to 21%, but in the next ten it had more than doubled to 43%. Between 2014 and 2020, the number increased significantly again, reaching 75%. It is a similar situation with the numbers for Democrats who view the Republican Party very negatively, although in every year but one the figures were lower than the Republicans.

Explanation: The clear upward trend shows that people in America are becoming more hostile towards their political opponents. This is evidence of significant and increasing polarization in American society.

3

1	depicts	6	sign
2	divided	7	corner
3	halves	8	foreground
4	separated	9	caption
5	background	10	tone

4

I think the artist's depiction of the Capitol is intended to convey the polarization of the American political system. The image of the divided Capitol with its large open space separating the two halves is a very strong image and reflects the huge differences between Democrats and Republicans. They are so far apart they cannot even communicate. The seriousness of the situation is evoked by the stark black and white colour and the prominent shadows. The caption refers to the annual speech made by the US president to the Houses of Congress and the point of the cartoon seems to be that the state or condition of the union is very bad indeed.

Writing workshop 1

1

26%: Gen Zers who do not believe they will be able to rely on social security in retirement.
31%: Gen Zers who think they'll have to work after retirement age
40%: Gen Zers who don't have any retirement savings.

2

line 1: direct address of the reader
lines 4–5: informal, humorous tone
lines 11–12: rhetorical question
lines 15 & 23: strong, emotive language
line 26: call to action

3

1	reflects	4	support
2	undermines	5	runs the risk
3	exaggeration		

4

Structure
The author uses a problem/solution style structure, e.g. the problem is today's Gen Zers will not be able to enjoy the same kind of luxurious retirement that currently older people do; the solution: start planning and saving now for retirement. EFFECT: engages readers and holds their interest so they are more likely to read until the end.

The author uses the introduction to establish a relationship with the readers. EFFECT: Readers will identify with the author; this is engaging and they will believe the author is on their side.

The main part consists of three paragraphs. In the first, the author shows how few GenZers have actually thought about their future. In the second, he/she gives information on the reality GenZers face. In the third, he/she presents the consequences of this reality. EFFECT: This structured and logical approach is more likely to convince readers.

In the conclusion, the author presents his/her advice to GenZers and ends with a call to action. EFFECT: A strong finish is more likely to achieve the result the author wants, e.g. that GenZers start planning and saving for the future.

Language – rhetorical/stylistic devices employed include:
Symbolism / Imagery: American Dream & happy ending in the title – evocative imagery that Americans identify with and is likely to encourage them to read the article.

Direct address / use of pronouns: "If you are anything like me …" (l. 1), imperatives "Look at those seniors …" (l. 5), "How many of you …? Have you even thought about it? Some of you have" (ll. 10–12), "Sociologists are describing us" (l. 16) "You know who you are!" (ll. 24–25). EFFECT: Readers will be engaged and will also view the author as a peer, meaning they are more likely to trust and listen to the author.

Informal register / humorous tone: Style: some contractions, e.g. "Do what I've done" (l. 26). Vocabulary: "an American 20-something" (l. 1), "oldies" (l. 3), "ugh!" (l. 5), "be poor, or something" (l. 24). EFFECT: The author's target audience, young people like him/her, are more likely to use this style and recognize the author as one of them – the chances are better that they will be persuaded.

Rhetorical questions: "How many of you …? Have you even thought about it?" (ll. 10–12) EFFECT: catches the readers' interest and holds it, because they want to know the answers.

Strong, emotive language: words such as "crucial" (l. 15), "NOW!" (l. 15), "little or no" (l. 22), "urgently" (l. 23), "at all" (l. 25). EFFECT: These increase the urgency of the issue and the impact of the author's message.

Factual evidence (argument by authority): "According to recent surveys…" (l. 12), "Sociologists are describing us…" (l. 16). EFFECT: shows that the author's message is not merely an opinion but supported by evidence so the readers are more likely to be convinced.

Illustration: see answers to exercise 3.

Writing workshop 2

1

1 Nevertheless
2 Despite
3 Although
4 but
5 however

2

Personal freedom: 66% of American adults believe the modern American Dream means personal freedom and the author says the modern dream is "a life of constant adventure … without a boss breathing down your neck, having total freedom" (ll. 9–10).

Religious freedom: In the graph, 56% of American say the dream means religious freedom, but the author does not mention this aspect at all in his/her description of the American Dream.

Equality: In the graph, equality is mentioned by 55% of Americans surveyed and the author focuses on it a lot. He/She says the old American Dream was only 'gettable' if you were "white and well-educated"

(ll. 15–16). He/She says inequality has less to do with race but has increased for many people (ll. 17–25).

Security: Security as in being safe from physical attack or danger is important to 54% of those surveyed, but the author only makes one short reference to Black people's security in line 18 when the Black Lives Matter movement is mentioned.

The pursuit of happiness: This is important to 53% in the graph and it forms the main focus of the whole article e.g. "enjoy the pleasures of life" (ll. 4–5), "live a life of constant adventure and passion" (l. 9), "modern American society … celebrates play" (l. 33), "living it large" (l. 66).

Economic freedom: This is the least important to Americans, according to the graph, but it forms a major part of the author's argument. The graph might correspond to the text in the following way: that Americans today are willing to accept a lack of economic freedom "living from hand to mouth" (l. 57), "acquiring more financial debt" (l. 59) in exchange for the (false) chance to live their "best lives" and being their "best selves" (ll. 61–62).

3

1 am writing
2 to start, asking
3 discussing
4 to consider
5 to say, providing
6 believe
7 reconsidering

4

1 poses, provide
2 states, previous, subsequently
3 repeatedly, overly
4 continues to be, purpose, bemoaning, require

5

Sir/Madam
I am writing in response to the article "Nothing more than a dream" which appeared in your newspaper on … .

As a young American, my view is that the author poses a lot of questions in this article but does not provide any constructive answers. For example, "Who wants a boring, stable job, when you could be having fun?" is asked but what the author is actually saying is not very clear. He/She repeatedly writes that the current generation of young people just want to have freedom and fun, but I believe this is overly simplistic.

The author states that the American Dream was "truly gettable" for previous generations but subsequently contradicts this claim by saying this was not true for a "large number" of Americans. The text spends a lot of time saying life was difficult for most people in the past and life continues to be difficult for most people today – I do not see any purpose in bemoaning that. We require more optimism, not less.

I would like to suggest reconsidering how we treat the subject of the American Dream. Dreams are by their nature unrealistic, but nonetheless they can serve to set a goal. In my opinion, we should spend less time talking about the dream being impossible for everybody and start examining what we can practically do as a country to help people achieve their own version of the dream.

As part of my suggestion, I believe strongly that we should look at ways of reducing the financial debt that young Americans like me have to struggle with before we even get our first job. The government, in my view, should take responsibility for that. Moreover, we should make new laws to protect workers in the gig economy so they are paid fair wages and have some security.

These are only two suggestions, but I think they are more constructive than simply criticizing the American Dream.

Brad Smith, Manchester

Dealing with listening tasks

1

2	20%	5	81%
3	3,500,000	6	26%
4	53%	7	a significant minority

2 a

1 remarks, a national   3 guns, supporters, just
2 politicians, polarized

2 b

4 self-defense: personal protection, defending/protecting themselves
40%: one in four, under half, a significant minority
one in twenty: 5%
5 over half: a majority, 50+%
state: say, feel, think
should: could, need to, must
6 present: current, today's
altered: changed
support: agree with, are in favour of, favour

3

1 an epidemic
2 gun law reform
3 one in five / 20% / one-fifth
4 for their employment / work / job
5 stricter / stronger
6 more liberal rules / more relaxed rules

Words in context

2

legislation: to legislate (vb), legislative (adj), legislator (n)

right-/left-wing
to conspire
to secede: secede
to condemn: Everyone should always condemn violence.
adversary: enemy, opponent, foe

3

1	numerous	4	vigilantes
2	revives	5	bill
3	denounce		

4

illegitimate, public discourse, bipartisan, insurrection, hostility, presidency

The chill out zone

1

Real: 1, 2, 4. Fake: 3, 5
Presidents: George Bush (Senior), Donald Trump, Joe Biden

2

1 second conditional   3 first conditional
2 simple past   4 present perfect

3 a

		¹G						⁴A
		E			³D			M
²L	O	O	P	H	O	L	E
		R			U			R
		G			G			I
		E			L			C
			⁵D	A	C	A		A
					S			N
⁶R	I	G	H	T	S			

3 b

Gorman

Topic 5

Getting to grips with grammar

1

1 had already returned – was born
2 came – had worked
3 lost – had spent
4 had seen – decided
5 had applied – learned
6 received – had classified
7 was – had shaken
8 had learned – decided

2

1	exactly	6	simultaneously
2	strong	7	clear
3	significantly	8	steadily
4	Interestingly	9	roughly
5	finely	10	slight

Dealing with visual material

1

1 a line graph
2 It depicts the number of EU and non-EU immigrants entering the United Kingdom between the years 2012 and 2019.
3 The graph comes from the UK Office for National Statistics and it was published by Statista in 2022.

2

1 From 2012 to 2015, EU immigration to the UK rose steadily, rising from just under 400,000 to around 600,000.
2 In the first half of 2016, EU immigration reached its peak at just over 600,000.
3 Following the Brexit referendum in June 2016, EU immigration to the UK declined gradually (from its peak of around 600,000 to 400,000).
4 In the second half of 2016, non-EU immigration overtook EU immigration / non-EU immigration increased while EU immigration decreased / non-EU immigration began to rise while EU immigration began to fall.
5 Since 2016 / From 2016 until 2019, non-EU immigration to the UK steadily increased.
6 Between 2017 and 2018, total immigration to the UK remained stable at approximately 1.1 million but the start of 2019 saw the beginning of a rise / an upward trend.

3

1 It is a pie chart.
2 It is divided into segments representing the percentages of non-British UK residents according to their region or country of birth.

4

1 Assuming the trends and figures in the graphs continue, Brexit seems to have had no effect in reducing total immigration. (This may be because non-EU immigration has been increasing and this is not affected by the UK leaving the EU.)
2 If the trend of increasing non-EU immigration to the UK continues, it is likely that the proportion of Asian and African immigrants will increase as EU immigration decreases.

5

support:
– the rise in hate crime shows that English and maybe British society has become more intolerant

– although the trend in religious hate crime is downwards the latest numbers are still four times as high as they were in 2011–2012
– the pie chart shows that around three-quarters of religious hate crime is against religions that are not viewed as 'traditionally English/British'

do not support:
– the pie chart does not tell us if the situation is getting worse or better; it only breaks down the types of religious hate crime in one year
– there is no definite link between the statistics and Brexit – it could be a coincidence
– the graph only shows information on England and Wales, maybe the situation in Scotland and Northern Ireland is not as bad

6

Lord Dubs, a British politician and someone who came to Britain as a child refugee, believes Brexit has made Britain a "meaner and nastier country". In this comment, I shall examine the arguments both in favour of and against this thesis.

Firstly, the rise in religious hate crimes in England and Wales began in 2012/13, as can clearly be seen in the line graph. This was the same time as the serious debate around Brexit in British society began and cannot be described as a coincidence. However, it must be pointed out that the statistics are only for England and Wales and do not include anti-Brexit nations such as Scotland and Wales. Consequently, we cannot say how strong the increase in hate crimes was in the UK as a whole. Furthermore, the figures continued to rise after the vote for Brexit in June 2016, reached a peak in 2018/19 and then began to decline significantly. If the rise were linked to Brexit, it could be argued that the peak should have happened in 2016 when the pro-Brexit side achieved its victory.

Next, the pie chart shows that at least 68% of the victims of religious hate crime are Muslim, Jewish, Hindu or Sikh. These are all religions that are not viewed as "traditionally British" by some people. Combined with the data from the graph, this points to a rise in intolerance and anti-immigrant feeling before, during and after the Brexit referendum. It could be argued, nevertheless, that the Muslim, Hindu and Sikh religions are not viewed as traditionally European either and Brexit was a debate around Europe so why would it cause intolerance against "non-European" religions?

To conclude, having considered the information in both graphs, I think it is hard to disagree with the opinion expressed in Lord Dubs' quotation. It seems clear that the debate around Brexit caused division and polarization in British society and allowed anti-immigrant feelings in general to be more strongly expressed, even in violent ways. While I agree with Lord Dubs that Britain has become "meaner", I hope the downward trend in hate crime shown in the graph continues and that the situation in Britain improves.

Writing workshop 1

1

acquit: to officially decide in a court that sb is not guilty of a crime

flesh: the human body

prosecution: the process of trying to prove in court that sb is guilty of a crime

vociferous: loud and confident when expressing your opinions

Victorian: connected with the period from 1837 to 1901 when Victoria was Queen of the UK

offence: normally an illegal act, but in the text a morally bad act

reckoning with: a time when sb's actions are judged to be right or wrong

sought to (vb. seek to): to try or want to do sth

set its face: to be strong in opposing sb/sth

acknowledging: accepting/admitting sth is true

2

1, 3, 5, 6

3

2 The text describes how some 19th century British authorities such as in Bristol thought people like Edward Colston, a 17th century British slave trader, should be honoured for their actions. (30 words instead of 41)

3 One of the text's arguments is that the jury's decision shows the British public are aware that public monuments can send old-fashioned messages with 19th century values. (27 words instead of 45)

4 The author does not think the "Colston Four" case gives everybody permission to cause damage to all public memorials because the issue in Bristol was unique and longstanding. (28 words instead of 45)

4

The summary should include the following in your own words:

<u>Historical background</u>

how 19th century public authorities such as those in Bristol positively viewed 17th century slave traders such as Edward Colston, despite the abolition of the slave trade in the 18th century

objections to Colston's statue were longstanding

many British buildings and monuments reflect outdated Victorian values

the history of the British Empire, and its religious mission to "civilize" the world, involved a lot of greed, cruelty and injustice

<u>Author's reasons</u>

the Colston statue was a unique case: it is not a "green light" to destroy all monuments; many people in Bristol objected to it for a long time; and the statue was wrong even when it was first erected – 12 years before it the city of Hull had put up a statue to someone who was against slavery

supports jury's decision as a sign that Britain is changing in a good way: the public are open to seeing that old buildings and monuments can send wrong messages

supports "good work" by the National Trust to educate British people about the negative side of the history of the British Empire

Writing workshop 2

1

A Let us examine this emotive issue.

B The cartoon evokes an image of an unhappy marriage and those often end in divorce.

C It is ironic that the arguments made by the anti-independence side sound a lot like the 'Remain' side in the Brexit referendum.

D Nevertheless, during times of wider global risks, the benefits of being a member of a multinational group would seem to be stronger.

E Timing, in my opinion, is the key issue.

2

Answers depend on student's opinions and research. Ideas based on the given graphs:

<u>'Dexit' pros</u>

In the last three years of the line graph, there was a decrease in the number of German people 'quite satisfied' with how democracy works in the EU. A significant minority (41%) of Germans were either not very satisfied or not at all satisfied.

Membership of the EU is very expensive: the bar chart shows that Germany pays the most of all members into the EU – €17 billion in 2018; more countries take money from the EU than give: 18 countries receive money, 9 countries pay money (10 including the UK)

Germany has significant non-EU trading partners (38% of trade) which could be developed.

<u>'Dexit' cons</u>

One in every two Germans is either quite satisfied or very satisfied with how democracy works in the EU, according to the line graph. That is close to a majority.

The EU is by far Germany's most important trading partner, according to the pie chart. Germany does over four times as much trade with the EU than China and almost six times more trade than the USA. Leaving the EU would affect this in important ways because of new taxes and costs.

Although it is expensive for Germany, the money it pays in is supporting other countries and improves the lives and economies of all Europeans. (bar chart)

Dealing with listening tasks

1

1. to lose sth that you want at the same time as trying to get rid of sth you don't want
2. sth that can be clearly seen to exist; sth practical
3. to do sth for sb to show that you are sorry for sth unfair or wrong that you did
4. to admit that you are responsible for sth bad or wrong
5. the complete possession of sth / sth that only belongs to one group and cannot be shared
6. the most important or successful part of sth
7. to have a lot of work or problems to deal with

2

exploitation, genocide, reparations, plantations, colonies, slavery

3

1G, 2A, 3D, 4E, 5B

Words in context

2

to commit sth: committed
confidence: to confide (v), confidence (n), confident (adj), confidently (adv)
to gain sth
publication: to publish (v), publication (n), public (n), public (adj), published (adj), publishing (adj), publicly (adv)
reparations
racial: race (n), racism (n), racial (adj), racist (adj), racially (adv)

3

campaigner:	● ● ●	(to) present:	● ●
monarchy:	● ● ●	reparations:	● ● ● ●
presumptuous:	● ● ● ●	scandal:	● ●

4

1. average person on the street
2. gathering steam
3. broad section of society
4. staged a protest

The chill out zone

1

True: 1, 4, 6, 7   False: 2, 3, 5, 8

2

the British Isles – Wales – the United Kingdom
Northern Ireland – England – Great Britain

Topic 6

Getting to grips with grammar

1

Not usually used in the progressive form: be, doubt, have, imagine, know, love, prefer, understand
Progressive form: become/becoming, cry/crying, decide/deciding, die/dying, plan/planning, rise/rising, stand/standing, travel/travelling

2

1. was – 2. were waiting – 3. tried – 4. were standing – 5. raised – 6. was searching – 7. screamed – 8. spat – 9. followed – 10. was walking – 11. could – 12. were doing – 13. had to – 14. was becoming – 15. was – 16. attacked – 17. were taking – 18. took – 19. managed

3

2. Nazeem has loved fashion since he was a young child.
3. He has been going to fashion shows since 2010.
4. Fashion magazines have published three of Nazeem's articles since 2020.
5. Nazeem has been writing a new article for two hours.
6. He has been searching for an internship in fashion publishing for two weeks.

Dealing with visual material

1 a

A in the upper left corner	F in the centre
B at the top	G on the right
C in the upper right corner	H in the foreground
D in the background	I in the lower / bottom left corner
E on the left	J at the bottom

1 b

The photo depicts a scene which takes place outdoors in a large garden maybe. Trees can be seen in the background as well as parts of a lawn and some bushes and shrubbery. Three people can be seen. There is a woman in the centre of the photo, facing towards the camera. She is a humanist minister and she appears to be performing a same-sex wedding ceremony. Facing her but with their backs towards the camera are two grooms holding hands. The groom on the left is wearing a dark grey suit and has short brown hair, a little longer at the back. The groom on the right is shorter than the other groom and his hair is darker and shorter, a little curly.

2

A oval
B triangular
C square
D rectangular

E cylindrical
F circular
G irregular
H jagged

3 b

The … cartoon is <u>made up of</u> two horizontal <u>strips</u>. In the first frame, we <u>see</u> two people … it is difficult to <u>tell</u> if … the man <u>is talking</u> to … we can <u>only see the man</u>. … he is <u>unsure</u> how to … without <u>causing</u> offence. … the cartoon zooms out to <u>reveal</u> that the man <u>is standing</u> … Now we know the person is <u>also</u> a man … he <u>prefers</u> to be called 'Mike'.

3 c

The message of the cartoon is clearly that non-disabled people can sometimes forget that people with disabilities are people first. Their names should be used as with any other person.

I believe the point the cartoonist is making is that even in basic social situations – like meeting people – people with disabilities have to have a lot of patience with non-disabled people.

The cartoonist might be trying to convey how non-disabled people can become confused by the different terms used to describe people with disabilities.

I think the cartoonist wants us to see how the non-disabled man sees the other man only in terms of his disability. He doesn't want to offend the man but because he sees the disability first and not the person, he probably causes offence anyway.

3 d

I think the cartoon is very effective in conveying its message for the following reasons:

The fact that we see the disabled person's head in the first frame, but we do not see him again until the last frame arouses our interest and successfully sets up the "punchline" in the last frame.

The contrast between the talkative non-disabled man and the silence of the non-disabled man is particularly effective in conveying how non-disabled people can ignore non-disabled people – the disabled person 'disappears' for two frames – and not respect them, even without meaning to.

The cartoonist's use of irony – by showing how complicated the non-disabled man makes the issue of talking to a disabled person while the disabled person simply wants to be called by his first name – made me stop and think. It made me reflect on my own behaviour and attitude towards disabled people.

Writing workshop 1

1–4

1c, 2e, 3e, 4b

5

a The case refers to the fact that high social mobility is more to do with strong families and social networks than financial wealth.

b The paradox is that meritocracy is supposed to mean letting people succeed through their own hard work and abilities, but we cannot do nothing – for meritocracy to actually work, we have to help it by helping create a sense of common good.

6

Answers should include the following:

<u>Author's view of social equality in Britain today</u>

Today's society is not very meritocratic. The author cites data from the Institute of Fiscal Studies, the Sutton Trust and the British Government's Social Mobility Commission to illustrate that inequality has become worse and social mobility has decreased in recent times.

Statistics on inequality now: richest 10% of households have five times the wealth of 50% of all households; working-class people are only 6% of doctors, 12% of top business management, 12% of journalists

Rich communities are among the worst places for disadvantaged students to live.

Poor communities can show high levels of social mobility (because of strong families and social trust).

<u>Improvements to society</u>

Efforts must be made to support meritocracy by focusing on building social networks and supporting communities – through membership associations and clubs, for example.

Government should be motivated by the common good to give individuals the best chance to achieve their potential.

Successful people should remember those who supported them and give more back to their communities.

Everyone must work together more to lift everyone up.

Writing workshop 2

1 b

Section B

Agreeing

- Women make up only a quarter of representatives in parliaments around the world (p. 281)
- Rape and sexual slavery are used as weapons of war (p. 233)
- The effects of climate change have a worse impact on women and girls (p. 233)
- Women gymnasts have to wear sexualized costumes when competing (p. 235)
- Olympic Committee is dominated by men (p. 235)

Disagreeing

- Women's participation in parliaments around the world has doubled in the last 25 years (p. 281)
- Attitudes are changing – team doctor in the US was jailed for sexually abusing women and girls (p. 235)
- Ibtihaj Muhammed – first female Olympic athlete to wear a hijab while competing (p. 235)

Section C

Agreeing

- Negative attitudes to asylum seekers in Ireland (p. 236)

Disagreeing

- Positive integration of asylum seekers in Ireland shows attitudes can change (pp. 237–238)

Section D

Agreeing

- 45% of LGBT students still face bullying in British schools (p. 242)
- 40% of LGBT students were never taught anything about LGBT issues in school (2017) (p. 241)
- UK government has to fund training for teachers to help equality in schools become a reality (p. 241)
- Vocal minority tries to divide society with its intolerant attitude towards LGBT people on religious grounds (p. 242)
- Women still only earn 77 cents for every dollar earned by men – the gender pay gap won't be closed until 2055 (p. 280)
- 70% of the world's poor are women (p. 280)
- Women do three times the amount of unpaid work looking after children and the elderly as men (p. 280)
- Financial services are biased towards men (because in AI only 26% of workers are female) (p. 281)
- Only 10% of states are led by women (p. 281)

Disagreeing

- Celebrations of the pride movement and the pride flag are now common and very positive (p. 240)
- Progress in marriage equality since 2001 when the Netherlands was the first country to officially certify same-sex marriage (p. 240)
- In celebrity culture, actors and musicians such as Laverne Cox and Lady Gaga promote equal rights and diversity (p. 240)
- New regulations in the UK mean children can learn about diverse relationships (p. 240 and pp. 241–242)
- 60% of British people want primary school teachers to teach children about non-traditional family types (p. 241)

Section E

Agreeing

- In British education, working class students still receive a lower quality education than middle or upper class (p. 245)
- The gap between rich and poor is greater than 30 years ago (p. 245)

- In the UK, 88% of children attend state schools but only 40% of the elites and 52% of MPs have a state school education (p. 246)

Disagreeing

- Over half of British MPs had a state school education (p. 246)

Section F

Agreeing

- People with disabilities are the largest minority group in the world but are often left out of the discussion around diversity and inclusion (p. 248)
- People with disabilities are 50% less likely to get a job than non-disabled people (p. 248)
- Even well-qualified disabled people earn $21,000 less per year than qualified non-disabled people
- The UN says that accessibility for people with disabilities is still a "major challenge" (p. 251)

Disagreeing

- There are good examples of famous people who overcame disabilities: Simone Biles, Prof. Stephen Hawking, Greta Thunberg and Jamie Oliver – ADHD, Asperger's, dyslexia and motor neurone disease are much more well known (p. 247, p. 255)
- Companies which are identified as being welcoming of disabled employees have a 28% higher revenue than other companies (p. 249)
- "Krip hop" movement in the US is a positive sign of more diversity in music, etc. (p. 250)
- The UN and western countries such as the US, the UK and Australia now have important conventions and laws around rights for people with disabilities (p. 251)
- Cities such as Melbourne, Australia, and Seattle, US, are showing how cities can benefit from being more accessible

2 **a**

1A, 2G, 3F, 4D, 5C, 6B, 7E

b

2 Yes, I will admit the world is far from perfect, but you must say that we have made a lot of progress, especially in the last few years. … (consistent formal style)

3 start new paragraph before "Now, let me move on …" (separate paragraphs for separate ideas)

4 The representation of women in parliaments of countries around the world has doubled over the last twenty-five years. (sentence structure)

5 Admittedly, this increase has brought / brings the percentage … nevertheless it shows we are moving in the right direction. (tense)

6 married to somebody … a reason for optimism (vocabulary)

7 If you are a person with a disability, I think the world today is a lot better than it was. I believe advances in technology … In my opinion, the fact that … (using synonyms)

3

Answers will vary although based on the evidence from the student's book alone (see answer to exercise 1b above), there is far more evidence in support of the quotation than against it. A good comment will however present the different aspects of the topic in a neutral way before reaching a conclusion in the final paragraph.

Dealing with listening tasks

1 b

diversity, LGBTQ, prejudice, ethnic, inclusivity

2

1 One-third
2 Black or Asian workers did not get employment opportunities.
   They did not get promotion in their jobs.
   LGBTQ+ workers suffered greater levels of harassment/bullying.
3 Include hairstyles in anti-discrimination legislation.
4 They are paid less than white women.
   It's larger now than in the past.
5 The general trend is towards more equality.
   Recent changes to the law mean inclusion and equality are required.
6 Everybody should tackle everyday discrimination. /
   Challenge negative attitudes from family, friends and colleagues.
   Business should have more women, people from LGBTQ+ and ethnic minorities in senior management.

Words in context

2

to face sth
compassion: compassion
expressed: to express sth (vb), expression (n), expressed (adj), expressive (adj), expressively (adv)
inclusion: to include sb/sth (vb), inclusion (n), inclusivity (n), inclusive (adj)
roughly: approximately, around, about
supported: to support sth/sb (vb), support (n), supporter (n), supported (adj), supportive (adj)

3 a

a2, b1

3 b

<u>bow</u>
verb: [baʊ] to bend over from the waist as a mark of respect or to acknowledge applause
verb: [baʊ] to move your head forward and down as a mark of respect or to show you are ashamed
noun: [baʊ] the front part of a ship
noun: [bəʊ] a weapon to launch arrows
noun: [bəʊ] a knot tied with two loops

<u>content</u>
noun: ['kɒntent] the things that are contained in sth, e.g a book or a box
adjective: [kən'tent] satisfied with what you have
<u>frequent</u>
verb: [fri'kwent] to visit a particular place often
adjective: ['friːkwənt] happening or doing sth often
<u>minute</u>
noun: ['mɪnɪt] one sixtieth of an hour
verb: ['mɪnɪt] to write down what people say in a meeting as a record
adjective: [maɪ'njuːt] extremely small
<u>second</u>
determiner/adverb: ['sekənd] happening or coming next after the first in a series
noun: ['sekənd] one sixtieth of a minute
verb: ['sekənd] to publicly support sb's suggestion
verb: [sɪ'kɒnd] to send sb to a different job than their usual job, normally for a short time
<u>tear</u>
verb: [teə(r)] to damage sth by pulling it apart
noun: [teə(r)] a hole in sth made by tearing it
noun: [tɪə(r)] a drop of liquid that comes out of your eye when you cry
<u>wind</u>
noun: [wɪnd] air that moves due to natural forces
verb: [waɪnd] to have many bends and twists; to wrap or twist sth around sth; to make a clock or a machine work by turning a knob or handle

4

1 for	4 between
2 from	5 with
3 about	

The chill out zone

1

1D, 2E, 3A, 4C, 5B

2

Culture: Stereotypes, native speaker
Gender and sexuality: attendant, they
Physical and health matters: people, condition, lives
Race: heritage
General: unique

Mock exam

Listening

1

1B, 2E, 3D, 4C, 5F

2

1 *Three aspects only from:* integrate, mix with the British, talk/act/eat like they do, don't be different
2 He lost more of his Jamaican identity,

3 She didn't take it – she stayed Jamaican,
4 Integration is easier than struggling (against racism), the Windrush Generation fought so the children wouldn't have to.
5 Jamaican culture was influencing (mainstream) British society.
6 His jokes were based on everyday racism.
7 *Three aspects only from:* be true to himself, celebrate his Black Britishness, make his comedy more inclusive, make all Britons laugh together.

3

1c, 2b, 3a, 4c, 5a, 6b

Reading and writing

1

(Introduction)
George Monbiot's opinion piece "Captialism is killing our planet ..." was published by The Guardian on Saturday 30th October 2021. In the text, Monbiot sets out his critical view of society's current approach to climate change and proposes a solution, all of which I shall now summarize.

(Main part)
The author begins by pointing out what he sees as an important difference between human beings and other living animals, namely, living animals put their survival first whereas human beings minimize dangers to their survival or, worse, even deny that the dangers exist at all.

He goes on to support this view by explaining how human civilization depends on the planet's environment being in balance, but he says that despite our intelligence we are ignoring the warning signs that Earth's systems are on the point of breaking down. To support his view, he gives examples such as heat domes over North America, massive fires and floods around the world as such warning signs.

The author then says that our wealth is a root cause of the lack of a reaction to the threatening disaster. In his opinion, regardless of a desire to be green, if we have money, we spend it. As a result, the richest 1% of humanity are causing the most damage to the planet because their consumption is huge.

The author uses the example of Bill Gates, whose consumption he claims emits three hundred and seventy times the amount of carbon a normal individual should if we want to stop global heating going over 1.5°. Furthermore, the author says, the supposedly green solutions to climate change recommended by the very rich will not help the situation but make it worse, citing the example of biofuels as one of the worst causes of habitat destruction.

As a solution to this predicament, the author suggests the use of wealth taxes to prevent people from becoming too wealthy. He argues that imposing limits on private wealth will enable humanity to increase public wealth for everybody, for example, in the form of beautiful public parks, public infrastructure such as hospitals, transport systems, playgrounds and community centres.

(Conclusion)
The author finishes his article by adding another part to his proposed solution: that people withdraw their cooperation from the current destructive system of capitalism. He writes that the key to successful campaigns was known to protesters in the past, such as the suffragettes, and is known to current environmental campaigners such as Extinction Rebellion. This key, he concludes, is to disobey.
(410 words)

2

(Introduction)

In his opinion piece "Capitalism is killing our planet ...", published by The Guardian on Saturday 30th October 2021, George Monbiot focuses on the threat climate change poses to humanity's survival and proposes a solution, using various means to convey his message and convince readers of his opinion.

(Main part)

From the very first line of his article, Monbiot uses the pronoun "we" to include both himself and the readers as members of humanity by saying "It's that we always put our survival first." This establishes the author as being on the side of his readers, even though he sometimes seems critical of people, and focuses the reader's attention on the fact that the threat described in his article faces us all. Indeed, the author directly addresses the reader numerous times throughout the text, for example, "You might expect" (l. 15), "It scarcely matters how green you think you are ... If you have surplus money, you spend it." (ll. 19–20). In the concluding paragraph, the author returns to using "we" and "our" when proposing his solution. This use of direct address and pronouns means the reader is more likely to accept the author's message because they will feel they and the author are part of a team effort.

Although Monbiot's tone is serious throughout the text, he does employ sarcasm or irony at times to point out the stupidity of society's response to climate change. This can be seen in l. 3–4 when he says "we seem to go out of our way to compromise our survival" and in lines 15–16 "You might expect an intelligent species ... But that is not how we function". By using this tone, readers should have an emotional reaction to the article, increasing its impact.

The author conveys his status as an expert on the topic of his text by including information on how complex environmental systems function (see paragraphs three and four) and also statistics on Bill Gates' consumption and its estimated impact on the environment (see paragraph seven). Furthermore, in lines 32–33 he supports his proposed solution by linking it to the "limitarianism" concept of Belgian philosopher Ingrid Roheyns. The use of expert knowledge and other respected sources increases the author's credibility in the eyes of his readers.

Other stylistic devices employed by the author include repetition and parallelism. The author repeats "mega-consumer" (l. 21). Examples of parallelism can be seen in lines 18–19 when he writes "The main cause … isn't your attitude. It isn't your mode of consumption. It isn't the choices you make" and also in the final paragraph "The 19th-century democracy campaigners knew this, the suffragettes knew it, Gandhi knew it …". The rhythmic repetition here can add to the impact of the author's message and make it more memorable for readers.

[…]
(Conclusion)

In conclusion, George Monbiot has an urgent message for his readers: our human civilization faces a great threat and only our collective action to change how we distribute wealth can help deal with the threat. In order to convince readers to agree with him, the author employs a wide range of rhetorical and stylistic devices in his writing.

NOTE: *Other rhetorical and stylistic devices used in Monbiot's article but not mentioned in the sample answer include:*

Emotive language: impending or chronic threat, breakdown, crucial, crashes, drag others down, triggering, cascade of chaos, collapse, mass extinctions, etc. EFFECT: adds urgency to author's message, evokes emotional response from the readers, increases engagement.

Alliteration: cascade of chaos, closer to its critical, great global flickering, the signals that … spell, these signals swiftly, radically altering its relationship, redistribute the riches. EFFECT: increases the impact and makes the message more memorable.

Metaphor: Its outputs begin to flicker – a great global flickering, climatic morse code, history's most important lesson. EFFECT: helps readers visualize ideas and makes them easier to understand.

Imagery: triggering a cascade of chaos, wealth taxes strike at the heart of the issue, poverty line / wealth line, when we want to spread our wings. EFFECT:

anchors clear images in the mind of readers, increasing the impact of the message and making it memorable.

Contrast: our highly evolved consciousness that once took us so far, now works against us; two tonnes of carbon dioxide per person per year. But the richest … 70 tonnes; poverty line / wealth line; private sufficiency, public luxury. EFFECT: adds emphasis to arguments by contrasting different or opposite ideas.

Register and style: This text is unusual because it mixes an informal style (use of contractions: It's, we've seen) and formal style (uncontracted forms: there is not, we will only endure) as well as informal and formal vocabulary (informal: supercars, tweaks, trashed, etc.; formal: withstands all evidence, a different matter, etc.). It also combines specialist terms (equilibrium states, systemic environmental collapse, critical threshold, limitarianism) and everyday language (we seem to go out of our way, when we want to spread our wings). EFFECT: The text is understandable to a wider range of readers, from other experts to non-experts, from serious readers to more relaxed readers.

3 A
(Introduction)

In his opinion piece "Capitalism is killing our planet …", published by The Guardian on Saturday 30th October 2021, George Monbiot lays out a disturbing image of the planet on the brink of environmental disaster. The main cause, he says, isn't our attitudes but our money. I shall assess this and the statistics as presented in the accompanying graphic.

(Main part)

Monbiot makes some striking claims. Among them, he says that "the richest 1% of the world's people produce an average of more than 70 tonnes" (ll. 24–25) of carbon in terms of their footprint, equivalent to thirty-five times the amount individuals should emit if we are to avoid an increase of 1.5° in global temperatures. He goes on to say that Bill Gates' consumption creates 7,500 tonnes of carbon emissions! These claims are hard to assess when the author only references "one estimate" without naming any source.

The infographic, however, does support Monbiot's message as it is produced by the World Inequality Report 2022 as published by Statista. Interpreting the information presented in the infographic, it can be seen that North America's and Europe's combined carbon footprint is three-quarters the total of the rest of the world combined: 30.5 tons compared to 41.5 tons. While this does not compare the carbon footprint of an average individual to that of an ultra-rich person, it does point to the fact that the rich, developed West has a huge carbon footprint compared to the average in the rest of the world.

Returning to the quotation, I find it hard to dismiss attitudes when discussing climate change and the environmental impact of our behaviour. Seeing the statistics in the graph and how Europe has a carbon footprint twice the size of South America when both regions have similar populations, I can only come to the conclusion that our attitudes and consumption must be factors.

(Conclusion)

To sum up, I agree with the statement that our money and wealth do indeed play an important part in our impact on the environment, but I have to disagree with the statement that our attitudes are not a cause. If we want to prevent the worst effects of climate change, we need to change how we spend our money and our attitudes.

3 B

(Opening)

Sir/Madam

I was very interested to read "Capitalism is killing our planet …" by George Monbiot and published in your newspaper on Saturday 30th October 2021, and it motivated me to write to you.

(Main part)

I found the author's description of the current weather catastrophes in North America, Russia, China and Europe as climatic morse code spelling "mayday" as very dramatic and worrying. I hope that the ultra-rich, as the author calls them, read his article and understand the message he is trying to get across. However, I have to say that I think the message of the article is not entirely correct. Let me explain why.

In his article, Monbiot says it is not important how green we think we are, and he goes on to say that our choices and our mode of consumption are not the main causes of our environmental impact. I have to disagree. Everybody is affected by climate change – there is no 'Planet B' as the environmental protesters rightly shout. Consequently, everybody has to be part of any solution to the crisis we face – the multibillionaires such as Bill Gates as well as the average working-class person like me.

The risk that George Monbiot runs by writing such an article is that ordinary individuals might think that the way they treat the environment makes no difference compared to the huge impact of the ultra-rich. Why should the average person recycle when Bill Gates causes the same damage to the environment as 3,500 ordinary people?

On a more positive point, I support the author's concept of "private sufficiency, public luxury" and I believe a wealth tax on very wealthy people is a very good idea. However, these constructive suggestions are followed by more negative and potentially dangerous suggestions.

In some ways, the author blames the ultra-rich and the powerful corporations they control, but in other ways he seems to be laying the blame on ordinary consumers because we consent "to the continued destruction of our life-support systems". The solution, he says, is to be disobedient. In my opinion, that is not very constructive and it risks being understood as an encouragement to go out and destroy shops and banks.

(Closing)

In conclusion, I think the article serves as a wake-up call not just for the Bill Gates of the world but for all of us. I believe ordinary individuals do not have to 'disobey' the whole capitalist society we live in. We can influence corporations – by using our money to support green companies and fairtrade products, for example. The influence of one individual is tiny, but if we all act together, our influence will be powerful; if we all act together, we can teach humanity a new lesson in making a constructive change.

(Add your name and town/city here).